MW01048368

OPEN-MINDEDNESS
...AND OTHER LIES

OPEN-MINDEDNESS… AND OTHER LIES

AND THE CASE FOR CUNNING AWARENESS

Patrick M. Oakes

ISBN:13:9781530701476

To Colleen, my wife:
Many daughters have done nobly.
But you excel them all.
Pat.

CONTENTS

Wisdom shouts in the street,

She lifts her voice in the square;

At the head of the noisy streets she cries out;

At the entrance of the gates in the city

she utters her sayings...

Proverbs 1:20-21

FOREWARD

A friend once asked:

"You know what you taught me about the Bible?"

Before I could react, he added:

"…that I should never make the Bible say more than what it does."

I can live with that.

PREFACE

CUNNING AWARENESS

- The highest wisdom cannot be achieved in its absence…Aristotle
- God wonders if anyone has it. <u>Twice</u>! (Ps 14:2, 53:2)
- The O.T. prophesies Jesus will have it (Jeremiah 23:5),
- Jesus concludes the church is lacking (Luke 16:8).
- During the "End Times" those with it will shine like the stars of the heaven (Daniel 12:3).

INTRODUCTION

I'm the younger brother.

My older brother, Stan, had a genius IQ. Straight A's without trying. Then God got a hold of him…and he prayed for a ministry which would keep him on his knees. I guess that means being humble. He went on to raise over $50,000,000 as president of The King's College.

I grew up trying to measure up. To say I was annoying would be an understatement. But that made me competitive. So, of course, I prayed for a *God-sized* ministry.

But first…a detour.

After high school I went to West Point. I flourished academically but one day, after being "dressed down," I resigned my commission. And of course, I blamed God.

I was a mess. I got involved with bad company. I was convinced <u>Christian narrow-mindedness</u> was the problem. That summer I had seven car accidents and several felonies. If that wasn't bad enough, while awaiting sentencing, I violated my parole.

I told God I was finally ready to listen. Strangely, I still wasn't convinced He was real. But I could fact-check Him with His book, the Bible.

God's forgiveness was immediate and overwhelming. He heard my prayer. The judge gave me a "do-over." I pled guilty but after a couple years my record was whited out from all the books (expunged). I thought…why not do something" for God? Maybe as a medical missionary.

But there was still crap in my life. I went back to college…but my grades tanked. To make things worse, admissions had already finalized the incoming class. School was starting without me.

So I asked God what He wanted. Remarkably, in a "word of prophecy," He let me know…I <u>was</u> going to med school.

In the end, school did start…without me. But in the middle of the first day, I got a phone call. I was in.

I worked hard. My grades were excellent. After the first year someone anonymously offered to pay my tuition.

After graduation and residency, I did several tours in Africa as a missionary surgeon. And it was there that God planted seeds that would bear unprecedented fruit in my life.

In Africa, I operated on thousands. I helped translate the *Jesus Film* into Siswati. It's estimated that each new translation brings 70,000 souls into God's kingdom.

But I wanted more. You know, to go deeper. So I prayed for that…even if God had to "put me on my back."

Within a week I was really sick. The next two months were spent "on my back" reading Proverbs. When I later recovered I kept reading. What a fantastic book! In the first four verses alone, I found seven different kinds of wisdom.

Chokmah	Wisdom, skill
Musar	Instruction, discipline, chastening
Biynah	Understanding, discernment
Sakal	Wise behavior, wisely understand
'Ormah	Prudence, shrewd, crafty
Da'ath	Knowledge and perception
Mezimmah	Discretion and purpose

I thought of Solomon. Remember? In a dream, God promised to grant him a wish. As a kid this had fascinated me. I remember making mental comparisons to Aladdin and his lamp. Solomon, of course, asked for <u>wisdom.</u>

But which one? Now there were seven to choose from. Solomon's story grew up before my eyes. This was no Aladdin's tale. It was for the fearless, the mature, even risk-filled.

Solomon's dream is found in two places (1 Kings 3:9 and 2 Chronicles 1:10). Together with Proverbs 2:1-5 we discover he desired knowledge...specifically knowledge which sprung from wisdom and understanding.[i]

To get this, Solomon prayed to *shama'* God (1 Kings 3:9).[ii] This word literally means "to hear." But for the Jews, l*ev shama'* is something far deeper. It means "to hear and obey God's heart."

So that was my first step. I needed a heart that heard and obeyed God's heart.

That led me to a deeper study of Proverbs. I learned that when you *shama'* Proverbs, God promises the same wisdom and discernment He promised to Solomon.[iii]

"...to know **wisdom** (*chokmah*) and instruction, to discern the sayings of **understanding** (*biynah*)" (Proverbs 1:1-2).

Proverbs was vetting my life. Said another way...this wisdom thing can work both ways. That's because it depends on whom you *shama'* (Proverbs 9:6 and 13:20). God is not the only source of wisdom. About the other one, James 3:15 says, "This wisdom is not that which comes down from above, but is earthly, natural, demonic." Understanding that was my next step.

The final step was to embrace the gift of wisdom. It's actually the theme of Proverbs. And it's not hidden. God shouts it out. As Proverbs 1:20-21 says, "Wisdom shouts in the street, she lifts her voice in the square; at the head of the noisy streets she cries out; At the entrance of the gates in the city she utters her sayings."

God doesn't want His wisdom stuck in the church.

"Wisdom shouts **in the street**" (bold emphasis mine). It's for our homes.

"She lifts her voice **in the square**" (bold emphasis mine)[iv] It's for our businesses and schools.

She utters her sayings at "**the gates in the city**" (bold emphasis mine)[v] It affects law and government.

Together these form the story line of this book.

Chapter One (Marriage)	"She lifts her voice in the street [in our homes]" (Proverbs 1:20).
Chapter Two (Business)	"She lifts her voice…in the square [in the marketplace of goods]" (Proverbs 1:20).
Chapter Three (Genesis)	"She lifts her voice…in the square [in the marketplace of ideas]" (Proverbs 1:20).
Chapter Four (Evolution)	"She lifts her voice…in the square [in the marketplace of ideas]" (Proverbs 1:20).
Chapter Five (Ecology)	"At the head of the noisy streets [a confusion of voices]" (Proverbs 1:21a).
Chapter Six (Minding the Brain)	"At the head of the noisy streets [a confusion of voices]" (Proverbs 1:21a).
Chapter Seven (Politics)	"At the entrance of the gates of the city [the

	politics of change]" (Proverbs 1:21b).
Chapter Eight (The Five Fools)	"Fools despise wisdom and instruction" (Proverbs 1:7b).
Chapter Nine (Open-mindedness vs. Cunning Awareness)	"I, wisdom, dwell with prudence" (Proverbs 8:12).

Wisdom "shouts"? Really? If that's so, why don't we hear it? Solomon gives the answer: "At the head of the **noisy streets**" (Proverbs 1:21; bold emphasis mine). God's wisdom is shouted down by competing philosophies, entertainments, and in general, the busyness of our lives.

Our reaction to the "noisy streets" are best displayed by the "five fools."

Five Fools of Proverbs

Pethiy	Naïve, "open-minded"[vi]
Latson[vii]	Scoffers
Kesil	Insolence, arrogant
'Eviyl	Evil
Naval	Fool, idiot, stupid, dense

Proverbs 1:22 introduces three of them: the simple minded fool, the scoffing fool, and the insolent, arrogant fool. Elsewhere in Proverbs we discover the last two. They are the evil fool and the dense fool.

But their Hebrew definitions give a very incomplete understanding of who they are. This will make more sense as we discuss *pethiy*,[viii] the "open-minded fool" and one of the main reasons I wrote this book.

Open-minded Fool

The *pethiy* are not just naïve, to God they are foolish and open-minded: "The [open-minded] believe everything, but the sensible man considers his steps" (Proverbs 14:15).

When I was in rebellion, I became convinced I had to be more open-minded. I was seduced by wisdom from the Enemy. The result was a disaster. Like this verse I was open to believe everything. Compare this to the sensible man. God cries out, "How long, O open-minded will you love being open-minded" (Proverbs 1:22).

There is a consequence to open-mindedness. Proverbs 1:32 warns "the open-minded": "For the waywardness of the [open-minded] will kill them."

That should trouble you. "Waywardness," from the Hebrew, *meshuvah*,[ix] means to commit "apostasy," a forbidding action. This is more than just contempt for the church or rejecting God. It means one must first be a Christian and then make a willful decision to renounce and live in opposition to God.

But the next part is even more disturbing. Because *pethiy* modifies apostasy (*meshuvah*), it is the "cause" and not the "effect." And that means apostasy comes from open-mindedness, not the other way around.

"Open-mindedness" is often embraced by churches. And it's causing our children to abandon God. This is not wisdom from above. It is "earthy, natural, and demonic." In Proverbs 1:10 God gives an astonishing warning.[x] "My son, if sinners entice you, do not consent."

"Entice" is translated from the Hebrew *pathah*,[xi] the root of *pethiy*, which we just learned means "open-minded."

So now replacing "entice" with "open-mind" we read: "My son, if sinners [open-mind] you, do not consent..."

From this verse we learn that sinners have an agenda. You are their quarry. They want to deceive you, make you "open-minded." Already their desire for "open-mindedness" is powerful and unrestrained.

Just a few verses later we find the word **love** being used to describe that desire: "How long, O [open-minded], will you **love** being [open-minded]?" (Proverbs 1:22; bold emphasis mine).

This word "love" is translated from the Hebrew word, '*ahab*, a word which is used to describe an intense, sexual love.[xii] The "open-minded" love "open-minded-ness" the way a man would love a woman. Writing this I can already sense the enraged reaction of the "open-minded." I'm a bigot, narrow-minded, intolerant...and, of course, invincibly ignorant.

Let them stew for now. I'll get back to them.

Instead, shouldn't you be asking why our Enemy (Satan), wants you open-minded? What's his strategy? For that, let's look at John 10:10a: "...he comes only to steal and kill and destroy..."

Satan comes "to steal and to kill and destroy." Let's look closer and see how he plans to do it.

ONE

He said, She said

"Wisdom shouts in the street" (in our homes).

Proverbs 1:20

Zama glared angrily. Eyes flashing, he insisted his Bantu medicine was as good as our "Western" practice. But that same afternoon his words came back to mock him. Ten gleaming white bones protruded grotesquely from the wrinkled gogo's mummified feet. That was all that was left of what had once been toes. Tiny black cuts could be seen just above some rotting flesh...the telltale Bantu marks of the native treatment. She'd come in with sprained ankles. Now both feet were dead. I often think about Zama. His passion and sincerity excelled mine. But he was wrong.

****

After three years in Africa my wife, Colleen, and I returned to the States. We were glad to find a fabulous, vibrant church. It was pastored by two youngish, energetic pastors and its intimacy belied its massive size. But after a bit, questions began to arise about their teaching. One of them was about marriage. Who was the leader?

This is not simply a local question. Look at the popularity of John Bristow's paperback, *What Paul Really Said about Women, the Apostle's Liberating Views on Equality*. And for this same reason you can't broach a topic like this without a huge disclaimer. So here is mine. Historically, the Church said that the husband was the boss. Cultural wisdom disagreed venomously and with good reason. No one doubts the considerable injury that has been inflicted on women in the name of this doctrine.

With that said, let's hear what my pastors said.

Their Solomon-like solution…neither. Husbands and wives should lead together.[xiii] Moreover, the pastors had a powerful argument. It was based on verses traditionally used to recognize the husband as the head of the household.

> Wives, submit yourselves unto your own husbands as unto the Lord. For the husband is the head of the wife, even as Christ is the head of the church: and he is the savior of the body. Therefore as the church is **subject** unto Christ, so let the wives be to their own husbands in everything. (Ephesians 5:22-24; bold emphasis mine)

Let's look closer.

Argument 1: Study of the Greek word *hupotasso* ("**subject** unto Christ"), translated "submission" (bold emphasis mine).

My pastors taught that the Greek verb *hupotasso*, or submission, was in the middle voice.[xiv] According to the rules of Greek grammar, that meant a wife's submission was entirely voluntary.[xv] They supported this explanation by referencing other passages where human action is modeled after Jesus' voluntary choices "to give" up His life for us. For example, Galatians 2:20 uses the verb *paradidomi*, also in the middle voice, which means "to give." It states: "I have been crucified with Christ; and it is no longer I who live, but Christ lives in me; and the life I now live in the flesh I live by faith in the Son of God, who loved me and [voluntarily] **gave** Himself up for me" (bold emphasis mine).

[19]

Ephesians 5:25 also uses *paradidomi* to describe how God gave Himself up for the Church.

Middle voice. A voluntary "giving." Christ's sacrifice was voluntary. The conclusion is inescapable. For both of them, Christ and women, any submission that they do is completely voluntary.

Argument 2: Study of the word, *kefale*, "head" (of the household):

The pastors' second argument was also strong. They argued that the husband was never even supposed to be the "head of the home." They claimed that this confusion happened because Ephesians 5:22 was incorrectly translated: "For the husband is the **head** of the wife, even as Christ is the head of the church" (bold emphasis mine).

In this verse "head" is translated from the Greek word *kefale*, which they claim means "first into battle" or "foremost in position." They insist that in the instances when *kefale* is translated as "head," it refers only to a physical head and not to a place of authority. Consequently, in this verse, the proper translation for both Jesus and the husband would be sacrificial, literally "first into battle."

Argument 3: The Bible teaches that both husband and wife should be submissive to the other.

This final argument is often given first. It comes from the verse just preceding the discussion on husbands and wives: "…and be subject to one another in the fear of Christ" (Ephesians 5:22).

This verse appears fairly self-evident. We should, each of us, husbands and wives, be subject to the other. So at various times, either the husband or wife would be the one leading, that is, they would share leadership. Moreover, the placement of this verse just before the discussion about husbands and wives provides the necessary context and pre-conditions for a successful marriage.

Pretty tight argument. But…were they wrong?[xvi]

Uncomfortable? You know, checking out your spiritual leaders?

I have two words: grow up! Babies are cute. But not so much decades later and they're still crawling on the floor soiling their nappies.

Vetting teachers actually has a biblical precedent. Look at how first century Christians reacted to an itinerant teacher of their day. As Acts 17:11 says, "Now these were more noble-minded than those in Thessalonica, for they received the word with great eagerness, examining the Scriptures daily to see whether these things were so."

This passage is about the Bereans. They were fascinated by this preacher guy. But…and this is huge…they were gonna check him out.

But hold on…wasn't this Paul preaching to them? You know…Paul, the same guy who wrote half the New Testament. Yep, and they were checking him out to see if he got it right! Paul's reaction? He praises them…calls them noble-minded.[xvii]

So the next step? Let's go to God's Word and get noble-minded.

Argument 1: My pastors claimed the wife's submission was completely voluntary because *hupotasso* was in the middle voice. They said it was like *paradidomi* meaning "to give," describing how Jesus voluntarily "gave" His life for us (Ephesians 5:25, Galatians 2:20).

First claim: *Hupotasso* is in the middle voice.

Hupotasso in Ephesians 5:24 can be in either the passive or middle voice. In the passive voice she is made to obey, while in the middle voice it is her choice to obey. But neither option changes the meaning of Titus 2:4-5. These scriptures require that the wife be submissive (whether forced or voluntary) so that scripture would not be blasphemed.

If this sounds confusing, consider the same question with something more familiar. When you're driving in the city no one actually makes you obey traffic laws. It is completely voluntary. But if you voluntarily choose to break the law you are at risk of being ticketed. The fact is that this is pretty much true for every law, whether civil or criminal. It's always been voluntary. And since God gave us free will, it's also true for this commandment too.

Second claim: *Paradidomi* **was also in the middle voice.**

None-the-less, my pastors tried to support their point by claiming that *paradidomi* in Ephesians 5:25 and Galatians 2:20 were also in the middle voice.

But they were wrong in both cases. That's because neither verse uses *paradidomi* in the passive voice (Ephesians 5:25 active voice, Galatians 2:20 participle). [xviii]

Argument 2: My pastors also claimed that *kefale* only meant "foremost" or "first into battle." That means it could never mean "headship" or "chief." Following that logic, Ephesians 5:22 does not say that the "husband is the head of the wife." And that would mean that Christ wasn't the head of the church either.

> "For the husband is the head of the wife, even as Christ is the head of the church." [xix]

That would make Christ the "foremost" in the church…or maybe the "first into battle" of the church. Trying this on similar verses is likewise awkward, and at times, turns them into gibberish (i.e. 1 Corinthians 11:3).

Meanwhile not one of the Standard Greek lexicons agree with my pastors. It turns out *kefale* can be and is used to mean "chief," as in "headship." [xx]

Dr. Gunn was amazed by my pastors' claims. He called them patently absurd, reflecting a complete ignorance of the Greek. [xxi] [xxii]

Argument 3: Their last claim comes from Ephesians 5:21 which says "be subject to one another in the fear of Christ."

This argument stands or falls upon a one idea…that both verses discuss submission. They bolster that argument with its placement just ahead of the discussion on marriage.

<u>Still wrong</u>!

This claim is easily rebutted on the basis of categories. The first discussion (Ephesians 5:21) is talking about submission within the church body; while the second (Ephesians 5:22) is speaking about marriage.

But a stronger argument would be to simply apply this same claim to Jesus and the church. They insist that Ephesians 5:21 is the key to a proper understanding of husbands and wives in marriage. If so, then it would have to apply equally to marriage between Christ and the church. The inescapable conclusion would be that at various times Jesus would have to submit to a very fallible church (e.g. consider the Crusades, etc.).

I'm going to pull back a moment and break a pretty fundamental rule for writers. I need to react to my pastors' unsupported teachings. This wasn't a trivial slip-up. The stakes couldn't be higher. Moreover, exposing this deception was pretty easy. So either those guys didn't try or didn't care…or maybe they just didn't like the result.

And maybe that's where you are too. I mean, after all, how much could it hurt if we just got with the times…you know, were a little more open-minded about mutual submission in marriage? I mean, haven't women suffered enough?

Okay, let's consider that. What you're asking is really two questions. The first question: which is preferable…obeying God…or following what feels right? Ironically, this is actually the same thing Satan asked Eve in the Garden of Eden: "Has God said…?" (Genesis 3:1).

What the serpent was asking was, who are you going to obey here: God, or what feels good to you?

The second question is more nuanced. If wives *hupotasso* their husbands, will they suffer harm? Based upon your personal experience, you might answer, "Yes."

And there are cases where you would be correct. First, there is the unusual case where God is the one who allows us to suffer.

[23]

Scripture points out that He does this at times to draw us back.[xxiii] Sometimes suffering is how we learn His truth.[xxiv] Other times God permits suffering to see if we will still obey Him.[xxv]

But there is another, very different reason why women suffer with *hupotasso*. This particular reason is clearly against God's will. And we will shortly explore this thoroughly.

But first you need to ask yourself why Satan is so interested in having us do this his way. The answer is found in Titus 2:4-5: "Older women…[should] encourage the young women…[to be] subject (*hupotasso*) to their own husbands, that the word of God will not be dishonored."

Look at the last word: "dishonored." "Dishonored" is translated from the Greek word, *blasphemeo*, the word from which we get "blasphemed." Let's read it again: "Older women…[should] encourage the young women…[to be] subject (*hupotasso*) to their own husbands, that the word of God will not be [blasphemed]."

That's intense…blasphemy! Titus warns that God's word can be blasphemed when women are not subject to their husbands.[xxvi]

But if that's really true, why would anyone make up the idea of co-leadership in marriage? I don't have a clue. But making up religious rules can be very seductive. It appears spiritual, but God says that it is done by those who are far from Him.

> "Rightly did Isaiah prophesy of you hypocrites, as it is written: This people honor me with their lips, but their heart is far away from me. But in vain do they worship me, teaching as doctrines the precepts of men. Neglecting the commandment of God, you hold to the **tradition** of men." (Mark 7:6-8; bold emphasis mine)[xxvii]

Jesus condemns pastors and churches who follow made-up rules rather than the Bible; He calls them hypocrites.[xxviii]

Okay, fine, you get it. But you're still definitely not happy with this submission thing either. It doesn't seem very godly to defend abuse of women with scripture. I hear that. And we're going to get there. But

[24]

first I'd like to discuss a case where the husband's leadership was clearly wrong. It's the story of Sarah and Abraham: "…Sarah obeyed Abraham, calling him lord, and you have become her children **if you do what is right without being frightened by any fear**" (1 Peter 3:6; bold emphasis mine).

What an odd verse. When I first read it, it made no sense. So I memorized it. It's found right after a discussion about husbands who aren't listening to God. 1 Peter 3:1-2 says: "In the same way, you wives, be submissive to your own husbands so that even if any of them are disobedient to the word, they may be won without a word by the behavior of their wives, as they observe your chaste and respectful behavior."

These verses explain that husbands may be "won" as wives submit to them. And that's when you find my odd verse. "Sarah obeyed Abraham…and you have become her children **if you do what is right without being frightened by any fear**" (bold emphasis mine).

But what does it even mean? It seems nonsensical, right? Let's take a look.

Sarah was amazing. In the story, twice her husband Abraham (then called Abram) passed off his wife Sarah as his sister, just to save his own skin (Gen. 12, 20). Both times Sarah (then called Sarai) submitted, even though Abraham exercised dangerously bad leadership. And both times, God protected Sarah, even when the local king took her into his harem.

Think of it. Because she obeyed, Sarah got stuck in the king's harem. Twice. Both times this happened because of Abraham's lie. But even though Abraham was wrong, Sarah submitted. Sarah was fearless (1 Peter 3:5-6). And God praises her.

So what did her obedience accomplish? Just everything!

God was watching. He saw what Abraham did. And He saw how Sarah responded. And then He intervened. So what difference did Sarah's obedience (and God's protection) have on Abraham?

We see it years later when Abraham took his son Isaac up to Mt. Moriah to be sacrificed as required by God. Abraham was not the same man who lied about Sarah. Hebrews 11 indicates that a fearless Abraham trusted that God would even raise Isaac from the dead if required to guarantee Abraham's promised heir.

> By faith Abraham, when he was tested, offered up Isaac, and he who had received the promises was offering up his only begotten son; it was he to whom it was said, "In Isaac your descendants shall be called." He considered that **God is able to raise people even from the dead, from which he also received him back as a type.** (Hebrews 11:17-19; bold emphasis mine)

What had changed? Go back and re-read 1 Peter 3:1-2. Abraham had been "won without a word" by Sarah's submissive behavior.

Cool story…but what would have happened if Abraham treated Sarah like this today?

…Sarah would probably divorce Abraham.

…Abraham would remain deceitful and cowardly (1 Peter 3:1).

…Sarah would parent their son not to trust Abraham.

…Abraham would never obey God's strange command (Hebrews 11:18-19; Romans 4:13, 17; Acts 3:25).

…The story explaining how sinners could be justified by faith would not be told (Genesis 22:8, 14; Romans 4:3).

…a story completed when our sin was put on Jesus and His righteousness was put on us (Romans 5:8; Hebrews 11:19).

Okay, so what just is the woman's place? As you can see, it's complicated. Paul reminds us that both Adam and Eve were dependent upon the other (1 Corinthians 11:8-12). Certainly when Adam met Eve for the first time, he was smitten. He proclaimed, "this is essence of my essence and flesh of my flesh" (Genesis 3:23).[xxix]

But after they rebelled Eve was consigned to be ruled by her husband: "To the woman He said, "…[your husband] will rule over you" (Genesis 3:16).

But her obedience gets God's attention and activates His power to straighten out a sinning spouse (1 Peter 3:1). So by trusting God, she honors His word (Titus 2:4-5).

And now at long last we've returned to your question: how can we follow God's word when it appears that submission leads to abuse? The answer: we do it right.

But before I explain, remember, it's not biblical for me to demand that my wife submit to my authority.

The scripture is very clear. In the passive voice, the verb (*hupotasso*) submission becomes intransitive and means "to become subject to," "to subject oneself to." She is still the one who makes herself "subject to," not me.

Yes, I am to lead the household, but that doesn't mean I'm better than my wife. If anything, our relationship is more like Sarah and Abraham. Nor are my prayers more important to God. She is my equal and my joint heir. Read 1 Peter 3:7 if you disagree.[xxx]

This verse adds that she is to be engaged intelligently with my mind *(gnosis)*. And I'm to grant her special honor "as with someone weaker, since she is a woman."[xxxi] Moreover, I'd be an idiot not to listen to her. Proverbs 31:26 says of a virtuous wife: "She opens her mouth in wisdom."

When I listen, the Bible promises me an unending blessing: "The heart of her husband trusts in her, and he will have no lack of gain" (Proverbs 31:11). In fact, God has specifically chosen my wife to reveal His favor to me: "He who finds a wife finds a good thing and obtains favor from the LORD" (Proverbs 18:22).

So to begin…as Colleen's husband, I also must submit to God's plan for marriage. And therein lies the problem, because most husbands don't have a clue what this looks like. But we can get a glimpse by re-reading Ephesians 5:25: "Husbands, love your wives, just as Christ also loved the church and gave Himself up for her."

This passage separates real men from the pretenders. A number of similes are used to compare husbands and wives with Christ and the church: "**As** Christ loved the church and gave Himself up for her" (bold emphasis mine).

Similes compare two different things with like/as to give us a brand new understanding. St. Paul (the same guy we alluded to earlier) used similes to mark the exalted place of women in marriage. He explains that the bar was set by Jesus…and it's inconceivably high.

> …that He might present to Himself the church in all her glory, having no spot or wrinkle or any such thing; but that she would be holy and blameless. So husbands ought also to love their own wives as their own bodies. He who loves his own wife loves himself; for no one ever hated his own flesh, but nourishes and cherishes it. (Ephesians 5:27-29)

This passage explains that God assigns the husband as leader. But everything in this passage is for her benefit, not his. He is to nourish and cherish her, and to present her holy and blameless, in all her glory. By loving her, he is loving himself. This principle recalls a verse in Hebrews in which benefits directly follow submission to leaders: "Obey your leaders and submit to them, for they keep watch over your souls as those who will give an account. Let them do this with joy and not with grief, for this would be unprofitable for you" (Hebrews 13:17).

Like the overseer's job in Timothy, my job, as husband and protector (1 Timothy 3:4-5) is to help my wife become a "woman of many parts" (Proverbs 31:10).[xxxii] This means she may be a homemaker (v. 14-15). Or perhaps she'll track down bargains or run the budget (v. 14, 16, 20, 24). She might start a commercial farm, plant a vineyard (v. 16), engage in commerce (v. 13-14), or even manage a business (v. 24). She will be generous, attending to those who are less fortunate (v. 20-21). She will nurture her family and they will return her love (v. 21-22, 27). She will be strong, yet kind; powerful, yet wise (v. 26).

Understanding submission properly is the key to correct

leadership in marriage. As we study the Bible we discover three options. The first is traditional submission where the husband leads selfishly, ignoring God's commands in Ephesians 5 to love, cherish, and nourish his wife as he would his own body. A second more contemporary plan proposes mutual submission without a designated leader. The third is God's plan and reflects His desire to bless the wife through her submission.

Historically, traditional submission was practiced without regard to the wife. To our modern ear, this seems offensive because it had a tendency to become abusive. Today it is being replaced by a more contemporary plan of mutual submission. But the modern version is open to times when a wife doesn't trust her husband and does as she sees fit. The Bible cautions that by resisting her husband's leadership, she may actually blaspheme God's Word.

At the end of the day, God's plan for marriage stands in sharp contrast to these counterfeits. It calls for the wife to be submissive to her husband whose leadership reflects her benefit. As this table illustrates, God's plan leads to provision and protection for both husband and wife.

Marriage	God's Plan	Contemporary Plan (Mutual Submission)	Traditional Submission
Assigned benefits (to be loved, cherished, nourished)	•Wife assigned benefits in Ephesians 5:25-33	•Benefits not assigned	•Historically abusive
Prayer	•Both heard, joined prayer stronger Mtt.18:20	•Blasphemers not heard Prov. 28:9, Tit 3:4	•Husbands prayers hindered, see 1 Pet 3:1
Husband's holiness	•Enabled by wife, 1 Peter 3:1	•Husband remains unrepentant	•Husband remains unrepentant
Wife's holiness	•Enabled through husband, Eph 5:26	•No benefit promised	•No benefit promised
Wife cherished	•Husband freed to cherish her, Eph 5:29	•No benefit promised	•Not evident
Husband respected	•Wife directed to respect him, Eph 5:33	•No direction or promise	•Respect is often absent
Woman's talents	•Husband facilitates Prov 31, 1 Tim 3:2-4	•No benefit promised	•No benefit promised
Woman's character	•Husband facilitates Prov 31, Eph 5:26,27	•No benefit promised	•No benefit promised
Children	•Nurtured by both Prov 31:27-28, 1 Tim 3:4	•No benefit promised	•No benefit promised

As the wife bends her will to her husband, she honors him, instead of blaspheming God's word. This same humility is a powerful weapon to win her husband should he arrogantly disregard God's will. Her respectful ways free him to nourish and cherish her to become that amazing woman God created her to be. Proverbs 31 explains that this development would be marked by both her inner character as well as her evident accomplishments.

We are going to conclude with one more pearl taken from Ephesians 5:25: "Husbands, love your wives, just as Christ also loved the church and gave Himself up for her." This verse explains that the husband's "giving" is meant to flow out of love for his wife.

In a mysterious way, this passage echoes God's love for mankind: "For God so loved the world, that He gave His only begotten Son, that whoever believes in Him shall not perish, but have eternal life" (John 3:16).

The only way for us husbands to love in this way is to imitate Jesus. To do that is a lifelong quest.

TWO

The Business of Heaven

"She lifts her voice in the square" (the marketplace of goods).

Proverbs 1:20

We'd agreed upon a price, but now the peddler was wavering. After years in southern Africa we were returning home. Our seven-day holiday in Mombasa was finished. The taxi driver waited impatiently as the peddler and I negotiated a new price for the beautiful malachite necklace.

"Did I have a T-shirt?"

My wife mused, "Methinks now he wants the shirt off your back!"

Two white T-shirts were added to my used Pulsar watch with built in calculator. The peddler's eyebrows arched imperceptibly. The transaction was complete.

****

BU$INE$$! It makes the world go round. It builds up communities and lifts nations out of poverty. It puts bread on the table, lets us buy houses, helps us put our kids through college, and allows us to save for retirement.

But hold on, there's a darker side, isn't there? Cue Pink Floyd's song *Money* with cash registers ringing in the background. Or roll a clip from Scorsese's filth-filled movie, *The Wolf of Wall Street*. Greed. Excess. Scams. Dissatisfaction. Ruin. Few topics can appeal to our gut like business and yet leave us queasy about potential pitfalls.

As a result, our relationship with business is fraught with tension. We find it respectable to hold a job, but what if it pays a multi-million dollar salary? Do entrepreneurs' innovative solutions justify keeping most of the profits for themselves? At the end of the day, are businessmen a corrupting influence or essential to our society?

The question that lays behind all these other questions is: how do we know what's right...or even more critically, what's wrong? Is it a question of performance and ability...or is fairness the issue? Each has its advocates. Some would argue that tensions between people would be resolved if we could just remove economic inequalities. Others grimly point out that past attempts to do this have not just crippled economies but resulted in increasingly oppressive societies.

Okay, so what does the Bible have to say?

That's a tough one. Even the church doesn't agree. Many believe it says nothing at all. Others believe if it says anything, it's that business creates inequalities that are the source of all evil. A third group believes that business is irrelevant to the Bible. This last group focuses its energy on the more "spiritual" questions of salvation and forgiveness. All three groups "lift their voices in the streets," desiring our allegiance. So...which is, right...and by that, I mean consistent with scripture? The short answer? None of them.

What?

Want to know what I think the Bible says? It's not hidden. The Bible is totally pro-business!

Okay, in today's culture that statement would not be just provocative, but flat-out imbecilic. Would it surprise you then, to learn that those are Jesus own words, beginning with "well done, good, and faithful?" [xxxiii]

Don't believe it? After all, it was that obvious, why doesn't everyone know it?

cHURCHY wORDS

Exactly the right question. Why don't people know? A lot of the fault belongs to the church. From early on, they spiritualized real-world passages. They did this by translating all the non-religious activities with "cHURCHY wORDS".

Such as?

Such as the word translated "steward" which actually comes from a Greek word, *economos,* meaning "business manager." *Therapeia* is translated "servants" instead of "service providers." Also overlooked are passages about wages, hiring, fraud, employee labor, debt, restitution, overwork, poverty, non-payment, investments, interest, prosperity, savings, success, co-signing loans, and bankers.

pARABLE OF THE tALENTS a.k.a. bUSINESS 101

So how do we get back to what God says? We start by looking at a passages that discusses the kingdom of God...which Jesus openly compares to business. Matthew 25:14-30 is the Parable of the Talents. Some grudgingly admit it touches briefly on business, but deny any deep connections between the two.

So as we begin, another disclaimer. This passage is plainly about the kingdom of God. But this makes my points stronger, not weaker. That's because the truth about the kingdom of God is encoded into the truth of what Jesus says about business.

That said, let's take a closer look: "For [the kingdom of heaven] is just like a man about to go on a journey, who called his own slaves and entrusted his possessions to them. To one he gave five talents, to another, two, and to another, one, each according to his own ability; and he went on his journey" (v. 14-15).

By looking at a similar account in Luke 19:12-27, we can see that this man has a specific title: "A **nobleman** (*eugenes*) went into a far country to receive for himself a kingdom and then return" (bold emphasis mine).

The man with 8 talents, or roughly $36.8 million, is a *eugenes*, a well-born man with royal connections. In the Luke account, he is even going on a business trip, to receive a kingdom for himself. He is what we would call today a high net-worth individual. Given his distribution of $36.8 million to his slaves for investing, we might call him an entrepreneur or a private capitalist. He makes things happen. He's a go-getter.

In a similar passage from Luke 12:42, while discussing business Jesus asks: "Who then is the faithful and wise **manager** (*economos*), whom his master will set over his household, to give them their portion of food at the proper time?" (bold emphasis mine). The word here for manager is *economos*, the root word for economics. The *economos* is not just a manager, he is a business manager.

Our private capitalist, the *eugenes*, shares similar qualities with the business manager, or *economos*. They are both managers. The private capitalist manages his capital and his financial investors. The business manager tracks food inventory and handles portion control.

Moreover, they are "faithful" in business transactions, the execution of commands, and the discharge of official duties. And they are both "wise" (sensible), meaning they are acutely aware of particulars: the ups and down of the market, the prices of different products, etc.

The passage in Luke 19 mentions owners' slaves, or *doulos*. They are by definition accountable to the *eugenes*. Moreover, they are vetted, that is, given fantastic sums of money, each according to his *dunamis*, or his power, based upon his abilities. Since we are looking at their fiscal responsibilities, we will refer to them in their capacity as financial investors. Adding what we now know, let's read the Matthew passage again in today's terms. "A high-net worth private capitalist was about to go on a business trip, calling his own financial investors and entrusting his capital to them. To one he gave $23 million, [xxxiv] to another $9.2 million, and to another $4.6 million, each according to his own ability, and he went on his trip."

Wait a second. This is the Bible, isn't it? What happened to the Sunday school language that we only half paid attention to anyway? This passage ain't having it. It's all about high-stake ventures. Business doesn't seem so marginalized anymore. Nor is it vilified or ignored.

The Bible doesn't stop at talk. It also calls us to action. We'll see that when we look at the entrepreneur's response to the performance of his investors. Before we do, let's round out the profiles of the investors, the "well done, good, and faithful" and the bad seed.

Immediately the one who had received the $23 million went and traded with it, and gained $23 million more. In the same manner the one who had received the $9.2 million gained another $9.2 million. But he who received the $4.6 million went away, and dug a hole in the ground and hid his master's money. (v. 16-18)

We see them plainly defined in the text: most successful, next most, and the failure. Let's look closer.

The top investor is entrusted with 5 talents, roughly $23 million, and invests with a 100% profit. He gets the lion's share of the capital and likely has prior experience testifying to his success in investing. My assumption is that he is similar to what we now refer to as a senior-level executive or investor.

The second investor is given 2 talents, or about $9.2 million, and is also a high-achieving investor. He isn't given quite as much as the first guy, but he does just as well, again with a 100% profit. Perhaps he is a mid-level executive on his way to senior-level status.

Our third guy is an outlier and that makes him a little harder to peg. He still gets 1 talent, or $4.6 million, which isn't exactly chicken feed. Is he a moderate-performing employee with room for improvement? Or a wet-behind-the-ears entry-level guy who is given his first big shot?

Let's start with what he does. He buries his investment. What significance does that hold? Well, it kept it safe from robbers. It also diminished his role as investor of that money. This guy literally rejected his charge to be responsible. If he had kept it, he might not have performed as well. But by burying it, he took away any chance for a positive outcome.

Okay! Now let's go back to when the entrepreneur returns to settle accounts with his investors, we get a close look of what "well done, good, and faithful" is.

> The one who had received the $23 million came up and brought $23 million more, saying, "Master, you entrusted $23 million to me. See, I have gained $23 more talents." His master said to him, "Well done, good and faithful investor. You were faithful with a few things, I will put you in charge of many things; enter into the joy of your master." Also the one who had received the $9.2 million came up and said, "Master, you entrusted $9.2 million to me. See, I have gained $9.2 million more." His master said to him, "Well done, good and faithful investor. You were faithful with a few things, I will put you in charge of many things; enter into the joy of your master." (v. 20 -23)

The private capitalist commends his first two investors with a special phrase: "well done, good, and faithful." The first descriptor is "well done." It is translated from the Greek word, *eu*, which means: acting well, to be well off, fare well, prosper. The praise directed at these investors stands in sharp relief to the derision heaped on businessmen today. The *eugenes* doesn't simply honor their business success. He praises them for the excellent profit they have made, a profit of one hundred per cent. But the word *eu* means very much more. Thayer and Smith's Bible Dictionary says that in addition to prospering, they acted well. This means that his investors did not sacrifice their integrity just to make money.

[37]

The second descriptor is "good" (*agathos*). This means to be upright, useful, of good constitution or nature, salutary, good, pleasant, agreeable, and joyful. This word describes both manager <u>and</u> product. Useful, of good constitution, and excellent describes the product. The businessman is to produce a product or service which has significant value and utility to the consumer. Distinguished, honorable, pleasant, agreeable, joyful, and happy clearly describe the person himself. How often do you see the news media applying these words to businessmen today?

The third descriptor is "faithful" (*pistos*). It means trusty, faithful in the transaction of business, the execution of commands, or the discharge of official duties. This word clearly identifies the Christian who chooses to engage in business as being both trustworthy and diligent. It is also a quality that the two investors share with their boss, whom we described earlier as faithful and sensible.

The private capitalist is just about to address the third investor. Their exchange shows just how seriously the *eugenes* takes the responsibilities he had handed out. Remember, it's not the investor's money. So he can very much be judged for how he handles it. Let's take a look.

> And the one also who had received the one talent came up and said, "Master, I knew you to be a hard man, reaping where you did not sow and gathering where you scattered no seed. And I was afraid, and went away and hid your $4.6 million in the ground. See, you have what is yours." But his master answered and said to him, "You wicked, lazy investor, you knew that I reap where I did not sow and gather where I scattered no seed. Then you ought to have put my money in the bank, and on my arrival I would have received my money back with interest. Therefore, take away the $4.6 million from him, and give it to the one who has the $46 million. For to everyone who has, more shall be given, and he will have an abundance; but from the one who does not have, even what he does have shall be taken away. Throw out the worthless investor into the outer darkness; in that

place there will be weeping and gnashing of teeth." (v. 24-30)

A nice churchy response would have praised the third man's caution and careful preservation of the wealthy man's money. After all, that's only fair. Instead, the private capitalist throws him out, and calls him wicked and lazy. The word used here for wicked, *poneros*, is the same one found in the Lord's prayer: "deliver us from *evil*." The second word, lazy (*okneros*) suggests not simply laziness, but loathing. The wealthy man sees through the charade. The third *doulos* loathes the wealthy man. His disgust is revealed by his sloth. It is his wickedness and laziness that leads him to bury the treasure in the first place.

After the rebuke, the wealthy man goes on to tell the investor he should have put the money in the bank, so it could gain interest. His final act is astonishing. In an act sure to give a migraine to today's social engineers, he takes the last servant's only talent and hands it to the one who already has the most. Something this amazing deserves its own chapter and we'll discuss it in more detail in the chapter "Hope and Change."

But this is not how most people would judge business. That's because most people don't give a rip about "well done, good, and faithful." Really? Why not? Because another phrase has caught their fancy and has become the mantra that defines our times… fairness.

fAIRNESS

Fairness! A very tricky word. So before we get lost in the opposing sides let's read what Matthew 20:1-16 says.

Our passage describes the head of a household (*Oikodespotes*)[xxxv] who in this scenario is similar to a modern-day recruiter. The head of the household went early to the marketplace to look for workers to labor in his vineyard. They agreed to a denarius for a day's work. The head of the household then went and looked for workers four more times that day. At the eleventh hour, he scanned the sparsely-populated marketplace and gathered up the few workers left.

With the work day at a close, the boss ordered his foreman to hand out the pay. The foreman didn't give preference to the first recruits. Instead, he paid the last guys first. And he must have slept through accounting class too, because he paid them a full day's wage for just an hour of work.

This isn't lost on the "early bird" workers. Mentally they're already spending the "windfall" wage they expect to receive from the foreman's fuzzy math.

> Now when those hired first came, they thought they would receive more, but each of them also received a denarius. And on receiving it they grumbled at the master of the house, saying, "These last worked only one hour, and you have made them equal to us who have borne the burden of the day and the scorching heat." (v. 9-12)

To call them unhappy would be an understatement. To them, this was decidedly <u>unfair</u>. They especially seem to bristle at the thought of the "eleventh hour workers" being their equals. They had an entitlement mentality and it shows. But the head of the household must have been expecting their reaction, because he has a response at the ready. He may have even orchestrated the whole scenario to provoke them.

> But he answered and said to one of them, "Friend, I am doing you no wrong; did you not agree with me for a denarius? Take what is yours and go, but I wish to give to this last man the same as to you. Is it not lawful for me to do what I wish with what is my own? Or is your eye envious because I am generous? So the last shall be first, and the first last. (v. 13-16)

fAIRNESS VS pAYBACK

To our modern ear, the foreman's actions seem unfair. Just what is God telling us? This passage seems even more baffling given Paul's requirement to bosses (masters) in Colossians 4:1: "Masters, grant to your slaves, justice and fairness, knowing that you too have a Master in heaven." This passage, while about slaves and masters, can be used to specify relationships between bosses and workers.

In the first case the boss seems high-handed and unfair while in the second we are told that bosses must act in justice and fairness. The latter case is highlighted by a warning: any breach would be judged by God. Taken together these two passages appear to sharply contradict one another. What is God telling us?

The answer is actually quite simple. Just ask of each if what they did was "well done, good, and faithful" (Matthew 25:14-30). From Jesus parable, did they honor the charge given to them? Did they act with integrity? Were they competent? Was their service valuable, bringing utility? Were they faithful, did they honor their commitments? Were they diligent?

In our first example, it is the employees who are being vetted. By asking the questions above it is clear that the workers were not interested in justice. Instead we see employee jealousy found masquerading as a call for fairness. Their intention is obvious: shaming their employer to subvert their contracts.

The second passage has no narrative. And it differs from the first by putting the bosses rather than the employees under the microscope. But like our first example it asks whether the boss's actions were "well done, good, and faithful." That standard is collapsed into the warning that they treat their employees with justice and fairness. This would include humane conditions with rest/food breaks; timely, complete wages without manipulation; rewarding special skills/work, protecting the vulnerable and responding to employee complaints without threats.[xxxvi]

The bottom line is that both cases are about justice and fairness. And both cases can be quite easily sorted using Jesus' own criteria, "well done, good, and faithful."

The topic of "fairness," together with its sister topic of "justice" will be revisited and amplified in a later chapter. So where does that put us?

wHAT dO wE kNOW?

- The words of Jesus: "Well done, good, and faithful" is the standard that scripture uses to judge business.
- Our modern notion of "fairness," used to judge everything from business to justice, is rejected as flawed and incomplete.
- Biblical "fairness" has a quite different look, a look reflecting "well done, good, and faithful."
- Jesus is an unabashed capitalist. If not, why would He use capitalism to describe the kingdom of heaven?

bUSINESS iN aMERICA

Using the biblical criteria ("well done, good, and faithful"), how does business in America measures up. How is that? Well, think about what American business does right...or wrong? Said another way, what would a "heavenly" best businesses and business ethics manual look like?

The simplest way to do this would be to spend time with our slacker investor. That would give us, at the very least, a picture of what our manual should and shouldn't look like.

- Should consider the cost of business prior to taking action.[xxxvii]
- Should recognize and prioritize seemingly random details to discern the "bigger picture," and then act quickly and responsibly.[xxxviii]
- Should act with diligence and circumspection. (a mind to work).[xxxix]
- Should be assiduous and careful with time and money.[xl]
- Should use experts when necessary to deliver a quality product.[xli]
- Should vet his employees and also have routine employee review.[xlii]

Our slacker investor slipped irresponsibly into sloth. He saw only the negatives of acting, never the consequences of inaction. He wasn't just given a slap on the wrist. He was kicked to the curb.

Warped by his perspective, the slacker's "cost of business" created delusions which became his new facts:

- His boss was unfair and intimidating.
- Investing was too hard or risk-prone.
- It wasn't his job to take care of the boss's money.
- His boss would confiscate any money he did make.

In sharp contrast, the success of his colleagues honored their boss. They understood, as Jesus said that "in this world, we would have many problems." They overcame the risks with diligence and circumspection. Moreover, they understood the concept of "wealth creation," using business money to create new wealth which then stayed with the company.

How could our slacker have considered the cost? By paying attention to details.[xliii]

- Would have seen his boss for who he is. Far from being a hard man, the private capitalist gave praise where praise was due, and criticism where criticism was due. He was not a hard man. He was a just man.
- Would have also had insight into the market. This would mean a better chance of finding a good investment, and options besides burying the money.
- Could have looked for expert help.[xliv] He wouldn't have to search far. The first two investors had plenty to offer.

After "counting the costs" and getting the details right, the next thing would be having "a mind to work."[xlv] This phrase is used by Nehemiah to describe Israeli exiles who were rebuilding the city of Jerusalem. Their single-mindedness overcame serious opposition both inside and outside the camp. It also enabled Nehemiah to strategize as he armed the workers to fend off violent attacks.

From there, the rest falls into place. Deliver a quality product.[xlvi] Invest in the engine of production over leisure.[xlvii] Avoid hastiness.[xlviii]

[43]

Avoid waste.[xlix] Pray for God's help.[l]

Finally, consider the <u>responsibility of riches</u>.[li] My brother Stan told me that when Harvard was endowed with a Chair for Business Ethics, they were initially stumped as to why businessmen should be ethical. Ultimately it was decided that they should be ethical because it was better for business.

Fortunately, the Bible has a bit more to say about this than Harvard. The businessman should treat both customers and employees with respect and integrity.[lii][liii] He was to act lawfully,[liv] and pay his debts/damages,[lv] and taxes.[lvi] And, considering the responsibilities of success, the businessman was to solicit God expectantly and thankfully.[lvii] Ultimately, the businessman was to keep everything in perspective and hold his heart carefully.[lviii]

Conclusion

The passage in Matthew tells us about the kingdom of God (Matthew 25:1-14). It records God's own voice as Jesus uses businessmen and business to characterize the "kingdom of God."[lix] The bottom line is that the truth about God's kingdom is encoded into God's truth about businessmen. Jesus couldn't use businessmen to provide insights into heaven if business itself was a corrupt enterprise. The practical implication of this is two-fold. If business can be corrupted, either directly by corrupt businessmen or indirectly through false libel then Satan can slander the truth about heaven.

Meanwhile, businessmen who follow God's plan should be honored not only for their excellent product but also for their integrity and hard work (well done, good, and faithful). And honoring businesses which are "well done, good, and faithful" brings honor to God.

THREE

In the Beginning: Part One

"In the beginning God created the heavens and the earth"

Genesis 1:1

Children are often the best motivators. A kid talking about a controversial topic can suddenly make it your top priority.

This happened in Africa when my five-year-old read a science book that could explain everything without God. It happened again when her brother was doing a paper on the two trials (Scopes and Dover) that book-end the evolution debate.

Their questions shook me. I decided to reread Genesis. See what it said about origins. I learned:

- That the universe was made after the earth (Genesis 1:2-16)
- That plants could live hundreds of degrees below zero (Genesis 1:11)
- That the sun wasn't necessary for the first part of the week. (Genesis 1:1-20)

Afterward I had an epiphany. Genesis made no sense.

****

Science and Nonsense

I'm not the first to notice this. Attempts by Christians and Jews to resolve these contradictions have included both literal and symbolic explanations. Some even think that Genesis One and Two represented two completely separate creation stories.

For example...

...in the "don't ask Mother Nature her age" category: Van Til (*The Fourth Day*) explained that the earth was billions of years younger than the stars. But Genesis said it was a full day older. So which one goes on her driver's license?

And on day three...

...you have plants. Who doesn't like flowers? But, wait a minute. The sun doesn't show up until day four. These must be very special plants because it's 4°K (-452.47°F) and the flowers not only refuse to freeze, they have no apparent need for photosynthesis.

And each day ends...

..."and there was evening, and there was morning, one day".

Evening/morning, evening/morning. If Shirley MacLaine had to chant a mantra from the Bible, this would be it. The funny thing is that when I think about evenings and mornings, I get a mental picture of the sun setting and rising. Setting/rising, Setting/rising. We're so used to our evenings and mornings that we may find it a bit shocking to discover that there wasn't even a sun until the fourth day. Nothing setting/nothing rising, nothing setting/nothing rising. But evening/morning for three days straight.

A bit nit-picky?

[46]

You think? Really! Are you aware that three out of four kids will leave the church after age 15?[lx] And you want to know why? Barna says a major reason is Genesis. To make sense of Genesis, our churches imposed a template on both its translation and meaning. The result is totally illogical. And that means your kids get hammered in school while defending church dogma. Do you want to know something? None of that ever had to happen. That's because when you strip Genesis of the traditional templates and English translations and look directly at the Hebrew the creation story is not only coherent but in fact, a scientific treatise.

But to get from where we are now to the original intent is quite a trek, so you're going to need some spoilers. The origins debate has a canon of literature with arguments from all sides. So allow me to be your shortcut-sharing guide for this chapter. You can bet I wish I had a cheat sheet when I first looked at this.

First Spoiler: The church is split. The division depends on how you translate "days." Seeing them as 24 hours like Seven Day Creationists, leads to 26-33 conflicts with science. Viewing them like Old Earthers, as eons of time results in irreconcilable problems of order. The solution is simple and is found in the Bible. And it supports both Seven Day and Old Earthers.

Second Spoiler: Science and Genesis have massive conflicts: the order problem, the light problem, the temperature problem, the morning/evening problem, and the translation/time problem. A few more are in the appendices: The Problem of Disorder, The Expanse/Heaven Problem, Chicken and the Egg, Both or Neither, Bunnies and Animal Death, Man's Unrest, Timing is Everything, and 199 Reasons to Believe.

Third Spoiler: Lost? A chronological map is found at the end of this chapter.

The truth is the church has been left behind. There's a lot of catching up. Let's start by looking at what the contenders say about my confusion.

Genesis

"In the beginning God created the heavens and the earth" (Genesis 1:1).

What a storied phrase. Moses, the author of Genesis, takes us through the days of the week, giving us both the order and description of what takes place. Having this degree of specificity should have eliminated questions about what happened and when.

But it hasn't. The question which lies behind every other question is what Moses meant by "days." How can there be three straight days, each with an "evening" and a "morning," without the earth (created on day three), or the sun (created on day four)?[lxi]

What do Seven Day and Old Earth Creationists say?

Unexpectedly, variations of the same thing. The missing sun vexes them equally. Both have to explain from Genesis, how a sunless planet can have evenings and mornings for three straight days.

Genesis vs. Seven Day Creationists

- Seven Day Creationists claim the first three days were based on the 24-hour rotation of the earth on its axis.
- They also believe that the earth was created on Day One.
- Both beliefs are refuted by Genesis.

The SDCs believe that the earth was created on Day One and then spun to create "rotatory" days. So without a physical sun, the first three days would be marked by the rotation of the earth on its axis every 24 hours. No sun was necessary since every 24 hours the spinning earth would create a day cycle.

Does the Bible say this? Nope, it's just speculation. But it's a necessary guess if the SDCs are going to explain why there are three evenings and mornings without a physical sun.

But their explanation has an insoluble problem. Evenings begin thirty minutes to six hours before sunset, while mornings begin just before sunrise and last until noon. The SDCs cannot explain how evenings and mornings happen for the first three rotatory days without the required sunrise and sunset.[lxii]

But there's an even more fundamental problem. Rotatory days cannot happen if there is no earth to rotate.

Genesis 1:2a says, "The earth was formless and void…"

"Formless" is translated from *tohu* (Hebrew). *Tohu* means "formless…of primeval earth, nothingness, empty space, wasteland. On the face of it this passage seems to say the earth did not exist. That would be consistent with how *tohu* is translated in Job 26:7: He (God) stretches out the north over empty space *(tohu)*.

Maybe Hebrew to English translators didn't like the sound of that. Who knows, but for whatever reason they instead translated it: "The earth was **formless** *(tohu)* and **void** *(bohu)*" (bold emphasis mine).

Using such obscure language has allowed traditionalists to then opine that this meant the earth was a "wasteland." That seems reasonable given that "wasteland" is a secondary definition of *tohu* (formless…of primeval earth, nothingness, empty space, wasteland…).

But somebody should have first checked out Isaiah 45:18-19. "… He is the God who formed the earth and made it, He established it and **did not create it a** *(tohu)* **waste place**, but formed it to be inhabited" (bold emphasis mine).

Wait a minute…the earth was a "wasteland" (commentaries on Genesis 1:2)…and the earth was not a "wasteland" (Isaiah 45:18).

Weird…okay, it's obvious both can't be right.

Let's first look at what Isaiah 45:18 was trying to say? When we look at the context, it's quite clear that "wasteland" is the only meaning which makes sense: "…(the Lord) established it and did not create it a waste place, but formed it to be inhabited…"

That being true, then *tohu* translated "formless" in Genesis 1:2 cannot refer to a wasteland, as many commentators say...otherwise the Bible would directly contradict itself.

For some, Genesis 1:2 will just have to remain a mystery. But I believe the meaning is quite clear and is reinforced almost a dozen times elsewhere in the Bible: the earth did not exist. As I just mentioned, this is consistent with how *tohu* is translated in Job 26:7. And it also fits with *tohu* from other passages: Job 6:18 (nothing), Isaiah 41:29 (emptiness), and Isaiah 49:4 (nothing). Moreover, it fits with how *bohuw* is translated in Isaiah 34:11 (emptiness).

And it's reinforced three times in Proverbs 8:23-29 which gives the creation story in both reverse and chronological order. It's also supported by Hebrews 11:3 and 2 Peter 3:5, which discuss both "eons" of time and the "not visible" "waters" of creation. But the capstone is found in Genesis 1:9-13.[lxiii] This last passage is indisputable because it describes the actual creation of the earth two full days later: "God called the dry land earth...There was evening and there was morning, a third day."

Obviously this entire last paragraph needs a much more detailed and leisurely explanation which I cannot do now. But for those who are interested it can be found in Appendix A: The Problem of Disorder and Appendix G: Timing is Everything.

Genesis vs. Old Earth Creationists

- Old Earth Creationists claim that the universe was created before the seven days of creation.
- That means the seven days merely explain things from man's point of view.
- Both claims are tempered by irreconcilable problems of order.
- OEs believe order is irrelevant because the days are allegorical or poetic or merely descriptive.
- That claim is refuted by Exodus.

OEs claim that the sun, moon, and stars were created before the Creation Week by the Big Bang. They point to the phrase "the heavens and the earth" from Genesis 1:1 as their proof: "In the beginning God created the heavens and the earth."

"Heavens and the earth" from the Hebrew *hashamayim we ha 'erets* is felt by scholars to be a merism, that is, a figure of speech representing the entire universe.[lxiv] According to them, Genesis then used the seven days to explain what happened from man's point of view. They have to do this because their interpretation leads to irreconcilable problems of order (see age of earth/sun above).

Consequently, anytime we point out a discrepancy in order they just fall back to Genesis 1:1 as creation. The days of the week are demoted to allegory, poetry, or simply points of interest. But this claim is clearly refuted by Exodus 20:11 which describes the creation as happening in six days: "For in six days the Lord made the heavens and the earth, the sea, and all that is in them, and rested the seventh day" (Exodus 20:11). Consequently, all future points with OEs will be discussed from that perspective.

The light problem

Closely allied to the earth/sun problem is the light problem.

> Then God said, "Let there be light;" and there was light. God saw that the light was good; and God separated the light from the darkness. God called the light day, and the darkness He called night. And there was evening and there was morning, one day. (Genesis 1:3-6)

God's epic command: "Let there be light." But just what is this light? It's tempting to say that it's the sun. But the sun wasn't created until day four. So if not the sun, then what?

The SDCs and the OEs each take their own approach on this one. First, let's look at the SDCs' position.

Seven Day Creationists and the Light: Two Possibilities

- SDC believe it was either a "special" light created for this time or the "glory of God (Revelation 21:25).

- Genesis dismisses the possibility of the sun or a star.
- And Revelation excludes the "glory of God" as a possible explanation.

SDCs believe that this was a "special light" prepared by God for this purpose. Maybe so, but we can immediately dismiss the sun, moon, and stars which weren't created until day four. Also any "special light" would have to heat the entire planet over 500^0 F. And even that wouldn't work without an atmosphere. It's noteworthy that none of the Bible's 31,102 verses supports such a light.

We can also exclude the "glory of God" possibility, described in Revelation 21:14-16 that lights the New Jerusalem. We know this because Revelation 21:25 explains that this special light will have "no night" as is explicitly required in Genesis 1:5.

Old Earth Creationists and the Light: Two Possibilities

- OEs believe the sun (or sun particles) was present on day one but couldn't be seen from earth due to dense clouds.
- But Genesis rejects the preexisting sun particle theory.
- And Job rejects a sun not visible because of thick clouds.

One argument given by OE's is that these verses don't refer to the creation of the sun, but a refashioning from pre-existing materials. They base that claim on a word study of "made" in verse 16 in contrast to the word "created" from verse one. Genesis 1:16 says: "God made the two great lights, the greater light to govern the day, and the lesser light to govern the night; He made the stars also" (bold emphasis mine). By contrast, Genesis 1:1 states: "In the beginning God created the heavens and the earth."

They explain that "made," from the Hebrew *'āśāh*, means that the sun was made from pre-existing material. The word "created," which comes from the Hebrew *bcārā'*, differs by suggesting that they were created out of nothing.

But that creates two problems. First, warming an ice cold planet ($+4^0$ Kelvin) more than 500^0F with little more than small particles. And second, this light must separate day and night, something we are told in Genesis is done by a fully developed sun (Genesis 1:14-18): "...Let there be lights in the expanse of the heavens to **separate the day from the night**..." (bold emphasis mine, Genesis 1:14, 16).

Old Earthers then shift their argument, claiming a fully functioning sun was present on day one but was obscured from sight because of thick clouds (Job 38:4, 9): "When I made a cloud its garment and thick darkness its swaddling band" (Job 38:9).

First, I'm not sure how this works since verse 16 says that the sun wasn't created until the fourth day. And second, how can a cloud canopy (Job 38:9) conceal the sun on day one when the canopy didn't exist until day three?

> Or who enclosed the sea with doors when, bursting forth, it went out from the womb; when I made a cloud its garment and thick darkness its swaddling band, and I placed boundaries on it and set a bolt and doors, and I said, "Thus far you shall come, but no farther; and here shall your proud waves stop?" (Job 38:8-11)

God tells Job that the thick cloud occurred during the creation of land and sea. From Genesis 1:9-10 we know that this would happen squarely on day three. There was no "cloud garment" and "thick darkness" on day one as described by Old Earthers.[lxv]

The translation/time problem

As I considered these puzzles, I thought of Dr. John Sailhamer, scholar on the translation team for the Holman and New Living Bibles and author of *Genesis Unbound*. He noticed that a particular phrase in Genesis One was understood completely differently elsewhere in the Bible.[lxvi] Later in Chapter Five we'll address other translation problems.[lxvii]

So what would happen if we looked just at the Hebrew? Even for a non-scholar like myself, the results were remarkable. Before we review my findings, let's agree on certain pre-conditions.

1. God created the universe and time simultaneously, as required by physics.

[53]

2. God generally speaks from our perspective. For example, when the Bible talks about the sun going down, it doesn't more accurately say "as the earth spins, the sun drops below the horizon."

3. Get rid of your preconceptions. Let the Bible speak for itself.

Traditionally the Church has considered the "days" in Genesis to be a length of time lasting twenty-four hours. But remember, time itself did not even exist until the universe was created. Moreover, there is no standard clock to be found anywhere in our cosmos.[lxviii]

That's why Jewish MIT trained physicist Gerald Schroeder asks, "When exactly would Man's Clock have begun?"

Shouldn't the answer be, not until man was created? So, before then, just whose clock would God have used? Wouldn't it seem both logical and reasonable that He'd just use His own clock? This is where the fun begins, because virtually everybody agrees that God's days consist of eons of time and are not bound by the 24-hour day rotation of earth's cycles.

God's Clock[lxix]

- Moses, who authored Genesis, also wrote a primer in Psalms to explain the language.
- God's days consist of eons of time and are of variable length.

Genesis says creation takes place in seven "days" (*yom*). That, together with evenings (*erev*) and mornings (*boqer*) is a strong argument to view the days as just that...twenty-four hours.[lxx]

Still, can we be sure? Look at Psalm 90 where Moses, the author of Genesis, created a lexicon to answer this question.

> "Lord, You have been our dwelling place in all generations. Before the mountains were born or You gave birth to the earth and the world, even from everlasting to everlasting, You are God. You turn man back into dust And say, 'Return, O children of men.'

For a thousand years in Your sight are like yesterday when it passes by, or as a watch in the night. You have swept them away like a flood, they fall asleep; in the morning they are like grass which sprouts anew. In the morning it flourishes and sprouts anew; toward evening it fades and withers away." (Psalm 90:2-6)

Four clues, all of which occur as similes. Recall that similes compare two very different things to give us a brand new understanding. They can be recognized whenever "like" or "as" is used to make that comparison.

Look at the first simile: "For a thousand years in Your sight are like yesterday when it passes by… "

"A thousand years" are roughly 365,000 days. But it says a "thousand years in Your sight are like yesterday." Two different things are being compared with "like" confirming this is a simile. Traditionally, the church believes this verse explains that God's days last eons of time (compare 1 Peter 3:8). What makes this interesting is the preposition that introduces the simile. The context is a reference to creation and to the transient nature of man.

"Eons of time" is not just some wild guess. These exact words are used by God to describe creation: "By faith we understand that the worlds (*aion/aeon*) were prepared by the word of God, so that what is seen was not made out of things which are visible" (Hebrews 11:3).

Don't see it? Me neither. That's because "eons" (the plural transliteration of *aion/aeon*) was purged in favor of a word less embarrassing to SDCs. Regardless, in both Greek and English, the language is clear, God's creation in Genesis took "eons of time" (see Appendix G: Timing is Everything).

A second simile from Psalm 90, reads: "for a thousand years in Your sight are like yesterday when it passes by or as a watch in the night." Three hundred sixty-five thousand days are being compared to both a full day or a very small part of a day. We already know that God's days consist of eons of time. Now we discover that His days also have variable lengths of time.[lxxi]

The final two similes from Psalm 90:5-6 are *boqer*, translated as "morning" and *erev*, translated as "evening": "in the morning (*boqer*) they are **like** grass which sprouts anew. In the morning it flourishes and sprouts anew; toward evening (*erev*) it fades and withers away" (bold emphasis mine)

Here, similes are being used to describe God's Clock. A thousand years are likened to the lifespan of grass. We see "sprouting grass" being compared to *boqer* (translated "morning") and "fading, withered grass" being compared to *erev* (translated "evening"). Remember, similes are used as a device to create a brand new meaning. In this case, Moses uses *boqer* ("morning") and *erev* ("evening") to describe the "beginning" and "end" of God's individual days.

Like God's days in Psalm 90, *yom*[lxxii] (Hebrew) translated "days" in Genesis can also refer to "periods" of time. Scholars agree that that's true even if you don't believe in "time dilation" (different clocks throughout the universe). Transferring the rest of what we learned in Psalms, Moses would be describing the "beginning" and "end" of God's day one, day two and so on.

That means *yom* is <u>both</u> a day <u>and</u> an "eon of time." It's a day when seen from God's clock. And it is "eons of time" when God's days are seen from man's perspective.

So what would change if you saw creation as "eons of time"? Nothing…and everything. Nothing, because it would still be God's story and it would still be a created universe. And everything, because God could use His own rules to cause the creation of the universe.[lxxiii]

But Seven Day Creationists object. They say Hebrew language rules demand whenever *yom* is numbered (1st day, 2nd day) it must mean 24 hour days. Even if their objection was correct (exceptions exist), they'd still be wrong. The "rules" only require this to be translated as "days" which could then represent either God's days or man's days.

By the way, it wouldn't change anything even if we still translate *boqer* and *erev* as "morning" and "evening" instead of "beginning" and "end." That's because the morning and evening of "God's days" would start and end at the extremes of the day. So from man's perspective, the morning and evening of "God's days" would be the same as the "beginning" and "ending" of "eons of time."

Looking at Answers

- The seven days of creation are God's days, not man's.
- From man's perspective, God's days represent eons of time and are not necessarily of equal length.
- Overlapping days can be confirmed by a careful reading of Genesis.

Given everything we have discussed—the order problem, the light problem, the translation time problem—Dr. Van Til's irksome "fourth day" question remains unanswered. How can you have "evenings" and "mornings" but no earth until day three and no sun until day four?

The solution itself is simple. Something happens on day three which will resolve not only this but will answer the question regarding the age of the earth relative to the sun and stars.

The days overlap. Yes, they are still sequential…day one begins before day two which begins before day three and so on. But they also overlap. The best way to get this is to think of someone making dinner in the kitchen. There are six separate tasks to perform. Each one is begun in a sequence, one through six. But any or all of the tasks can continue even after the next task is begun.

Want proof? Turn to Genesis 1:11-13 when all the plants were made: "Then God said, 'Let the earth sprout vegetation: plants yielding seed, and fruit trees on the earth bearing fruit after their kind with seed in them;' and it was so."

But some plants yielding seed did not sprout until much later.

Recall that Adam and Eve were created at the end of day six (Genesis 1:27). In Genesis 2:7-25 we learn that the Garden of Eden was created just after Adam but before Eve. But "plants of the field" could not sprout without the presence of both Adam and rain (Genesis 2:5). In Genesis 1:29 Adam and Eve are told that they can eat every plant yielding seed on the surface of the earth. Every plant yielding seed on

[57]

the surface of the earth would include "plants of the field (*sadeh* cultivated plants) which presumably yielded seed as they do today. That would mean they would be in the Garden (Genesis 1:29). And that, of course, would require rain (Genesis 2:5).[lxxiv]

But in Genesis 1:11 we are told that <u>all</u> sprouting of plants with seeds had to happen on the third day. How could some plants with seeds sprout on day three and others not until day six when Genesis says they all have to sprout on day three? I know of only one way. Day three would have to overlap with day six.

Overlapping days would resolve a number of things. It would explain how the earth, made late on the third day/period can be younger than the sun, made earlier on the fourth day/period. Recall that day three begins with the gathering of waters (primordial gases set aside for the earth) into one place. But since these are God's days, the earth does not necessarily have to happen in the first 24 hours or even the first 10,000 years. With overlapping days, stars created early on day four could be older than the dry land of earth created late on day three. This explanation fits <u>exactly with the scripture without doing damage to any of the text</u>.

Recall that without overlapping days the earth would be a whopping 454.5°F below zero. Cold enough for you? Plants would freeze in seconds. This is a <u>major</u> problem for Seven Day Creationists. Overlapping days also resolve the issue of plant photosynthesis. It is common knowledge for anyone who gardens that the sun is indispensable to grow green plants.

This is not to say that God could not have used instantaneous creation, a present explanation by Seven Day Creationists. But it isn't required and it doesn't fit the scriptures. At any rate, I don't really get their fixation on instantaneous creation. God doesn't always finish his work in an instant; the healing of Naaman's leprosy and the blind man from Bethsaida didn't happen instantaneously. Once again, this is not to say that God could not do it that way. He just didn't do it on day three with the plants.

Putting It All Together

- Empty space
- Cosmic explosion
- Waters above and below
- Earth, sun, moon, and stars

So what would this story look like if we were actually talking about God's day one, day two, and so forth?

Verse two of Genesis One reads "The earth was formless and void" from the Hebrew *tohu wa bohu*. Recall that *tohu* refers to "formlessness or empty space" and *bohu* refers to "void and emptiness." Dr. Schroeder believes the phrase, "formless and void" together with "darkness over the surface of the deep" refer to the unformed building blocks of the universe. This fits nicely with Proverbs 8:27 and Hebrews 11:3 where God prepared (*kuwn* "set up, prepare") the universe through *eons/aeons* of time from "things" not visible (see Appendix H Timing is Everything).

Directly following is God's epic command, "Let there be light." This expression compresses the primordial particles, initiating a cosmic explosion popularly called "the Big Bang."[lxxv] This fits with God "stretching" the stars across the heavens (stretching cannot be an instantaneous process).[lxxvi] God calling "the light day" is the creation of "time" itself. Day is translated from *yom*, meaning, of course, "day." But it also means "time" or "a period of time." This makes sense because "time" as a human construct did not even exist until the very moment of the creation of the cosmos.

God calls the light "good" from the Hebrew towb, in this context meaning with "good understanding." This is a critical quality, one deemed necessary by cosmologists who claim that the Big Bang had to have design built into it.

Immediately God separates the light from the darkness. Without either earth or sun, this is a problem for both SDCs and OEs.

But remember, Genesis was written in Hebrew, not English. It actually reads: God separated (*ben badal* "divided a space between") the light from the *choshek* ("darkness", also rendered metaphorically as "obscurity"). This *choshek* is called by God *layil* ("night" also rendered "protective shadow"). *Ben badal appears* to suggest we are talking about physical space (although it can also be used otherwise). "Obscurity" and "protective shadow" easily describe those regions surrounding the universe beyond the Big Bang. This understanding fits nicely with God's Clock and also resolves issues for both SDCs and OEs.

God's cosmic explosion creates a nearly instantaneous expansion of particles which separates "the waters from the waters." God calls this "expanse," "heaven" (Genesis 1:8). Talking to a non-scientific audience, Moses uses "water" to metaphorically describe the gaseous products of the "Big Bang." Using water to describe particles has been done multiple times in the Bible (Job 26:8, 2 Samuel 22:12, Psalm 18:11).

The "waters (or particles)" above and below represent the building blocks created by the Big Bang which God uses to form the stars above and the earth below. [lxxvii] This is supported by the use of *min* with both waters described. The Hebrew *min* means "out of (of material from which something is made)."

If you're interested to see what stakes SDC and OE people have in the expanse issue, turn to Appendix B: The Expanse/Heaven problem.

Before I conclude, I want to provide the straight-forward summary that I promised about the seven days of creation.

Straight-forward Summary: Seven Days of Creation Paraphrased

Genesis 1:1. In eons of time (Hebrews 11:3) God created (Proverbs 8:27 *kuwn*, "set up," Job 38:4-5 and Isaiah 51:13 *natah*, "stretched" i.e. not instantaneous) the heavens and the earth and this is how he did it.

Genesis 1:2. At first, there was no actual earth, only emptiness (*tohu wa bohu*, empty space (Proverbs 8:27, Isaiah 45:18,19, cp *tohu* Job 6:18, 26:7, Isaiah 41:29, 49:4 and *bohu* Isaiah 34:11).

This emptiness is where God places the primordial particles (described as the deep and the waters (Proverbs 8:27, Hebrews 11:3, 2 Peter 3:5).

Then God uses His power to draw the waters into a singularity (moving over the surface of the waters).

Genesis 1:3. Then God said: let there be a cosmically large explosion ("let there be light"), called be scientists today the Big Bang.

Look at Hebrews 11:3 …so that what is seen was not made out of things which are visible taken together with 2 Peter 3:5 …the earth was formed out of "water" and by "water." Recall that twice in other passages the Bible uses "water" to describe gaseous particles. Taken together we see invisible gaseous particles cosmically exploding, i.e. "the Big Bang."

Genesis 1:4. Fitting science, God attends (*ra'ah* Hebrew) this explosion so that it has design built into in (*tobe/towb* of good understanding).

God uses this act to separates the universe from those areas beyond (*choshek*: darkness or obscurity; Job 38:19).

Genesis 1:5. As science later discovers necessary with creation of matter, God simultaneously creates time (called the light day*: yom*, meaning day or time).

All of this describes God's first day, or from man's perspective the first vastly extended variable periods of overlapping time (Psalm 90:4-6).

Genesis 1:6. God commands the explosion to continue to expand outward (expanse in the midst of the waters) and fill the space with primordial gases (Isaiah 42:5, 51:13, Jeremiah 10:12, Hebrews 11:3, 2 Peter 3:5, see Appendix C Chicken and the Egg).

Genesis 1:7. God separates those bits which were to become the earth from those which would fill the universe (waters above and below, Proverbs 8:26-28, see Appendix A Problem of Disorder).

Genesis 1:8. God calls his universe "heaven".

This describes God's second day, or from man's perspective, the second vastly extended variable periods of overlapping time (Psalm 90:4-6).

Genesis 1:9. Next, God gathers the particles which were below into one place, drawing a circle on the deep (Job 38:8, Proverbs 8:27-28, Isaiah 40:22).

The circle represents the primordial particles on the primeval ocean which will become the earth, refuting the SDCs contentions that the earth was made before the deep.

Genesis 1: 9-10. After that God creates the land (Genesis 1:8-10, 10, Job 38:4-8, Proverbs 8:25-29, see Appendix C: Chicken and the Egg) and sea (Job 38:8-10) and a cloud canopy which encompasses our planet (Job 38:8-10). The canopy doesn't happen until Day Three refuting OEs claims it was present on day one, Job 38:9-11).

Genesis 1:11-13. God next commands the fruit trees and the plants with seeds to sprout, a process which continues until the sixth day (Genesis 1:29, Genesis 2:5, 8-9).

That confirms that God's third day would overlap with His sixth day. From man's perspective, the third vastly extended period of time must overlap the fourth, fifth, and sixth vastly extended periods of time.

Genesis 1:14-18. God creates the sun, moon and stars. But this does not mean that these luminaries were after the earth. It's like what we saw with the plants which sprouted from day three until day six. Because the days overlap, the sun and stars made on day four could precede the earth made on day three.

Genesis 1:19 (describing Genesis 1:14-18). This describes God's day four, or from man's perspective the fourth vastly extended period of overlapping time.

Genesis 1:20-22. God commands the waters to teem with creatures, and directs either birds or insects to fly above the earth. After giving this command, he creates sea monsters (dinosaurs), living moving creatures in the water, and winged-birds.

[62]

Genesis 1:23 (describing Genesis 1:20-22). This describes God's day five, or from man's perspective the fifth vastly extended period of overlapping time.

Genesis 1:24-25. God commands the earth to bring forth cattle, creeping things, and beasts of the earth.

Genesis 1:27-30. At some point afterward (still on day six), God creates Adam, followed by the Garden of Eden, and then Eve (Genesis 2:7-9, 21-23).

Genesis 1:29-30. The garden includes more sprouting as God's day three overlaps with God's day six (Genesis 2:5). They will eat every green plant and every tree with fruit yielding seed (again suggesting rain was present in the Garden of Eden (compare Genesis 2:5).

Genesis 1:31 (Describing activity of Genesis 1:24-30). This describes God's Day Six, or from man's perspective the sixth vastly extended period of overlapping time.

Genesis 2:1-3. Finally, God rests on His Day Seven, a rest which continues even today (Psalm 95:7, Hebrews 4:3-4). But that would mean His Day Seven has lasted for thousands of years, which, of course, contradicts Seven Day Creationists (for an expanded discussion read Appendix F: God's Clock and Man's Unrest).

Genesis 3:1-7. Of course, the creation narrative ends with Adam and Eve sinning early in their situation (see Bunnies and Animal Death in Appendix E). God curses the ground and says that man will eat plants of the field which are now choked by thorns. This again contradicts some Seven Day Creationists who insist that rain didn't fall until the flood, because plants of the field cannot sprout without rain (Genesis 2:5, 3:18).

This paraphrase describes the seven days of creation when seen from God's perspective. And it also describes the seven overlapping eons of time when seen from man's perspective.

Using both God's days and man's days together is consistent with other biblical passages, some of which even give mathematical models to compare the two.[lxxviii]

Creation of the Universe with all Five Creation Accounts

A description of the days of creation wouldn't be complete without incorporating details from every creation account. Throughout this chapter, we have mentioned five different creation accounts. Below, I explain how together they tell the story of Genesis.

Creation Events	Scripture	Action	Science
Original particles	Gen. 1:2	No earth, only "deep"	Primordial particles
Particles readied for Creation	Gen. 1:2	Spirit moving over the face of the waters	Particles drawn into singularity
Creation of expanse	Gen 1:3, Isaiah 45:12	Let there be light	Big Bang
Design of creation	Gen. 1:4	*Towb*/excellent, good understanding	Cobe condensation/design
Differentiation universe from regions beyond	Gen. 1:4	Creative explosion distinguished from obscurity	Universe set in context of non-universe
Creation of time	Gen. 1:5	Called the light *yowm*, time	Simultaneous creation of time/matter
Regions beyond universe	Gen. 1:5	Enclosed in protective shadow	Naming the unknowable beyond the universe
Beginning/ending God's days	Gen. 1:5	*Boqer/erev*	Sequential overlapping events
Separating creation of earth and stars	Prov. 8:26, Gen. 1:7	Expanse in midst of the waters	Particles set aside for earth/stars
Particles of universe	Gen. 1:7	Waters above	
Formed into shape of earth	Prov. 8:27	Inscribed circle onto deep	Angular momentum of sun spins off parts for earth

Creation Events	Scripture	Action	Science
Earth separate from universe	Gen. 1:7	Waters below	Naming particles of the earth
Invisible "waters" of creation	Heb. 11:3, 2 Pt. 3:5	Not made out of things visible	
Creation of land	Prov. 8:28	Made firm the dust above	Particles gravitationally condensed
	Prov. 8:26	Dust, then fields, then hills	Physical earth
	Ps. 104:6, 8	Small mountains	
	Job 38:8	Sea through doors from womb	Earth's core heat erupts water
	Job 38:16, cp. Gen. 7:11	Springs of the sea; recess the deep	
	Prov. 8:24	Springs abounding with water	
	Prov. 8:28	Springs of the earth fixed	
Primordial pan-ocean	Psalms 104:6, 9b	Land covered with deep	Pan-ocean over flat earth two miles deep
	Prov. 8:24	Depths	
	Job 38:9	Made cloud its garment	Creation of atmosphere
Creation individual oceans	Gen. 1:9	Waters gathered into one place	Tectonic plates and continents
	Prov. 8:29	Boundary for seas	

Closing Thoughts

My study of Genesis was much like an experience I had when my wife Colleen and I were taking a respite from mission work and vacationing in Ballito Bay just north of Durban, South Africa. It was a wonderful time with warm sunny beaches and a beautiful ocean view.

While there, I chose to swim far past the warning buoys which were placed for my safety. Beguiled by the waves I was well into the ocean before I realized I was being pulled further and further out to sea. I was in a rip tide, a natural phenomenon which has taken many an unwary swimmer. Within moments the land had become small on the horizon and fear gripped my heart. But I had been warned in the past not to fight this current because after a bit it would curl back toward shore. Just as my hopes dimmed, the current changed and I was pushed back toward the shore and safety. But as I got closer to land I realized I was going to be smashed against sharp lava boulders, just outside the safety buoys. My body still bears the scars from this misadventure.

Diving into the creation story, I expected to find a rich experience, supporting either the SDCs or the OEs, or both groups. Instead I found myself being pulled by Genesis further and further from my preconceptions. In my panic I decided to let scripture explain scripture, believing that God's truth would prevail. I was grateful when God's word began to bring me back to what I thought was my comfort zone. But instead of safety it brought me to a new place, one which wreaked havoc on my earlier bias. Seven Day Creationists were right when the creation week was seen from God's Clock and His point of view. But Old Earth Creationists were right when seen from Man's Clock and man's point of view. As I continued to study Genesis I was taken to a new place. Like those sharp rocks, this place inflicted further injury on my churchy notions, replacing them with a more biblical perspective. I had been wrong earlier when I thought Genesis made no sense. Now looking at the Hebrew, the creation story not only made sense but was, in fact, a scientific treatise and consistent with what I saw in nature.

FOUR

In the Beginning: Part Two

The marketplace of ideas

"She lifts her voice in the square"

Proverbs 1:20

"Daddy, I don't know if I believe in God anymore."

My brain raced as I listened to my eldest daughter, not quite six years old. We were barely six weeks into our mission work in Africa.

What should I say? Even though she was precocious, admitted to special classes in California, she was still a babe, literally not knowing her right hand from her left. I took a deep breath…then asked her what she meant.

Holding up a 6th grade science book from the States, she said:

> *"I was reading this book, and they can explain everything without God."*

I searched for a response. Everything seemed way too deep.

> "Honey, I'm going to teach you a word."

[67]

She nodded, secure in the innocent belief God grants little children that their daddies can fix anything.

> "Infinite."

Her eyes shone with confidence and understanding. I kept going.

> "Infinite means a number that never stops getting bigger."

Even as I said this I regretted my inadequate vocabulary. I was relieved when she nodded understanding. So I asked:

> "Honey, if you have 'infinite' sheep, how many chocolates do you have?"

> *"None, Daddy."*

I hesitated again. The words were getting bigger.

> "I have another word, 'contingency.' 'Contingency' means it came from something else. Like you. You came from me. I came from Grandpa and Grandma...and so on."

She nodded again. Remarkably her young mind had grasped the connection to her book where animals evolved into other animals. The latter was contingent on the former.

> "Okay, I have one last word. 'Necessity.' 'Necessity' means it didn't have to come from anything else; it always existed."

In the hot African sun, sweat dripped down my neck. This was too big a jump.

She nodded.

I relaxed slightly. Then I asked my final question.

> "Sweetheart, if you have 'infinite' 'contingencies,' how many 'necessities' do you have?"

As I deliberated how to finish the Kalam cosmological argument, my precocious daughter interjected:

"Daddy, how can they be so dishonest?

Surprising and audacious, my five-year-old had figured it out. Whether you have one contingency or an infinity of them, it remains just that…a contingency. It gives you no beginning. All you've done is push the question back. Where did it all come from? We are still waiting for their answer.[lxxix]

****

You already saw what happened in Chapter Three, where we let scripture explain scripture. This chapter is how I think it happened. Bear in mind that this represents only one possibility. And while my explanation is completely consistent with scripture, it does not share the same strength as what is explicitly said in God's word. Moreover, since what follows is my opinion I do not want to be misunderstood or misquoted. That is why I must now emphatically insist that it is in no way whatsoever an endorsement of evolution.

Evolution…to speak of the theory is problematic. Which one? Darwinian, synthetic (neo-Darwinian), punctuated equilibrium, Goldschmidt's monsters, the law of biogenesis, the neutralist or selectionist models, prebiotic evolution, panspermia, self-organizing genes, various cosmological models including steady state, oscillating, Big Bang with Cobe condensations, infinite multiverses, theistic fellows like Dobzhansky, or even agnostic evolutionists who would embrace anything but what we now have. You can take your pick.

But after careful review I have concluded that there are two features which are common to all of them.

Understand that I am deaf to any protests as I intend to remove any technical language and/or biological doublespeak.[lxxx]

The first feature is the notion of <u>time</u> and <u>chance</u>. It is both elegant and powerful.[lxxxi] It is not to be improved upon. Briefly stated, this says that given enormous <u>time</u>, animals evolve into other animals through random, <u>chance</u> events.

The second is that despite the bewildering display of possible explanations for evolution, every single one is moved across <u>time</u> and <u>chance</u> by the engine of natural selection.

It would, therefore, be safe to safe to say that if the engine of natural selection failed, evolution itself would be dead in the water. So let's examine the principle working parts of this engine.

1. Thomas Malthus said that too many animals are born for all to survive.
2. That being so, Herbert Spencer has said that the fittest will survive.
3. Darwin concluded that if the fittest survive they will pass on traits and form new species.

Over the protests of evolutionists, I will maintain that that is a tautology.[lxxxii]

Tautology? What's that? Tautologies are pseudo-scientific arguments that are always true by definition. It's kind of like saying that your father is deaf because he's hard of hearing.

Okay, so what's that got to do with natural selection? Let me answer your question with a question. Which ones survived? That's easy, the fittest. How do we know they were the fittest? Simple, they survived. Do you see it now? It's always true by definition. But what happens to the argument when we remove the tautology and say it again? Survivors survive. Therefore, one animal becomes another. Really?

****

A New Story

Paleontologists have found over 30 phyla in the Burgess shale from the Cambrian period. In the Linnaean taxa (classifications of plants and animals), the phyla are the categories just below the animal and plant kingdoms.[lxxxiii] The Burgess Shale is known to have essentially every phylum present today. Evolutionists who first encountered this explosion of life often remarked that it was just like special creation. By this they meant that these phyla then created all life "after their kind" as in this representation:

Linnaean taxa:

- (Linnaean taxa are now encompassed by 3 Domains)[lxxxiv]
- Kingdom
    o Plants
    o Animals
    o Four additional categories
- Phylum (In the old Linnaean system change in fossils seen here for evolution)
- Class
- Order
- Family
- Genus
- Species

Even in the modern context the evolutionist's remark, "after their kind" sounds familiar, a lot like Genesis. But "young earth" Christians strongly resist the possibility. They insist that the biblical word *(miyn)* translated "kind" can only mean species.

Their understanding would look like this:

Linnaean taxa:

- (Linnaean taxa now encompassed by 3 Domains)
- Kingdom
- Phylum
- Class
- Order

- Family
- Genus
- Species (change happens here, producing all of life; e.g.: Dobermans and Poodles) [lxxxv]

Meanwhile, Dr. Terry Mortenson from the scholarly "young earth" organization *Answers in Genesis* more accurately translates *miyn* as "families" for animals and "families" or possibly "orders" for plants. Diagrammatically this would look like this:

Linnaean taxa:

- (Linnaean taxa now encompassed by 3 Domains)
- Kingdom
- Phylum
- Class
- Order (change in plants possibly happens here, producing all of plant life)
- Family (change in animals and possibly plants happens here, producing all of life)
- Genus
- Species

I consider the change by Dr. Mortenson from *Answers in Genesis* from "species" to "family/order" for the word translated "kind" (*miyn*) to be legitimate. But I also find it instructive. *Answers in Genesis* no longer believes that change "after their kind" refers to "species," For Dr. Mortenson, change "after their kind" now refers to "families" for animals and "families" or possibly "orders" for plants. But what biblical source did *AIG* use to determine this new definition of the word "kind" (*miyn*)? And what biblical source did they use to exclude the other taxa?

When I look at how *miyn* (after their kind) is used elsewhere in the Bible it is attached to specific animals. But in Chapter One of Genesis it modifies broad generalities, i.e. beasts of the earth. A straight-forward reading would suggest that when used with specific animals, "after their kind" refers specifically to that animal. Could it be that when used with larger groups, "after their kind" refers to changes within the larger group, i.e. phyla? That would fit exactly with what paleontologists are finding in the Burgess Shale.

Linnaean taxa:

- Linnaean taxa are presently encompassed by 3 Domains
- Kingdom
- Phylum (biblical change here or in domain, producing all of life)
- Class
- Order
- Family
- Genus
- Species

But you say that this sounds like theistic evolution. Absolutely not. Theistic evolution does believe that life was set in motion by God. But then, like atheistic evolution, it believes that change across kinds occurred randomly by chance.

This is not simply a technical point. Chance to an evolutionist means that change can <u>never</u> be directed intelligently. But I believe that the story of creation is neither random nor non-rational. God commands various groups to reproduce "after their kind." All changes within the kind happen in response to His command and according to His rules.

But how can something follow the rules and still appear random? Consider when someone jumps from a plane. No one knows where they'll fall. It appears random. But because of <u>God's law</u> of gravity they <u>will</u> fall.

I will add that God could have even used the methodology of natural selection. After all, a creationist, Edward Blyth, came up with a form of natural selection to support God's creative plan two dozen years before Darwin (of course, Blyth's focus was different than Darwin's).

Once again, for some of you this is a deal breaker. But I want you to consider something. Everyone (atheists, OEs, even SDCs) accepts natural selection when we discuss species (or now, for *Answers in Genesis*, at the "families/orders" level). We see it every day: animal breeding; genetic manipulation of crops; antibiotic resistance in bacteria.

What creationists balk at is natural selection outside of "species" (or now, "families/orders," see discussion above). Their reasoning is that God made species (or "families/orders") reproduce "after their kind." Okay, fine...but the word "species" (or even the Linnaean "family/order") is <u>never</u> actually used in the Bible...not even once. Not ever. Nada. So they have no reason to resist an alternative explanation for *miyn* via the phyla of the Burgess shale.

But maybe you might think that this overturns what I said earlier about tautology. Not at all. It actually adds a second barrier for the evolutionist.

Barrier One

Natural selection <u>is</u> a possible methodology for change "after their kind." My problem is that evolutionists use natural selection to validate natural selection. That's like having your kid write his own excuse for violating curfew, or a doctor give his own second opinion.

To show why this fails, consider this <u>analogy</u> which uses the same methodology.

We observe that careless lovers get pregnant.

Now think of pregnancy as an engine of change, changing careless non-pregnant women into careless pregnant women. I'm calling this "careless selection." Now use your engine of change to validate itself by locating fossils of pregnant women. Even if you could find such fossils, the argument could never prove anything.

The argument will always be flawed for two reasons. First, you are using the engine of change, pregnancy (or the fossils of pregnant women), to validate itself. And second, it doesn't account for pregnant lovers who were careful.

Nor would it help the argument if, like the evolutionists, you change the wording from "careless selection" to "differential reproduction of careless pregnant women as a function of ethnicity that has a genetic basis." Ditto for alternative terms like "improved design, heritable characters, fitness, and reproductive success."

Similarly, Darwin's "natural selection" fails. It uses the engine of evolution to validate itself. It doesn't differentiate between selection done intelligently in response to God's command and selection done by chance. Consequently, the argument remains flawed no matter what language you use (i.e. "differential reproduction, etc.").

Here's a second illustration. We had said at the beginning of this chapter that evolution was a tautology, that is, a pseudo-scientific argument that is always true by definition. We had said that would be like claiming that the reason your father is deaf is because he is hard of hearing. It's important to note that this statement does not necessarily mean that the father is not deaf. It just means that this statement is always true by definition.

So what's missing? Our little scientific friends, verification and falsification.

- Verification: like an audiologist (<u>independent criteria</u> to show the father really is deaf)
- Falsification: performing a critical study to evaluate other possibilities of deafness (like ear wax)

Barrier Two

The second barrier for evolution to overcome is that natural selection is not specific to either evolution or special creation. Consequently, its mere presence does not advocate either. The critical difference is that evolutionists insist that this is a non-directed, random event whereas creationists believe it is an intelligently directed methodology.

In summary, we have considered Genesis 1 and 2. By looking at the Hebrew text we were able to eliminate apparent contradictions seen in the English translation. Based upon the Hebrew, I have proposed a hybrid explanation (uniting seven day and old earth creationists) which is textually accurate and is supported by scientific evidence.[lxxxvi]

The bottom line is that this is God's story, not ours. We cannot know for certain whether God's creation was instantaneous or a process following His rules. Any of the Christian explanations has more explanatory force than the theory of evolution. So whether God used a literal seven-day creation with man's 24 hour days, an "old earth" process, or as I presented, a combination of both, we need to guard against arrogance and skepticism. Arrogance…denouncing other Christians when God's truth is not entirely clear,[lxxxvii] and skepticism…dismissing Genesis One and Two because we don't fully understand it.

FIVE

The Soul and Make-Believe

…And why it's important to the environment

"At the head of the noisy streets" (a confusion of voices).

Proverbs 1:21a

In western Africa our water came from the roof, trickling down into a large cistern. Colleen boiled it twenty minutes, then ran it though a ceramic filter. We prayed over it too, thinking of the bloated rodents floating in our water supply.

At night, I immersed myself in Swahili, needed for communication at the hospital I worked at four mountains distant. I was grateful for the Hurricane lantern during the times we had no electricity. To break up my language study, I would read Tempels' *Bantu Ontology*, one of three books on the otherwise bare shelves in the library. Ontology, in simple words, is the study of the soul.

The book was about animism, widely practiced in Africa. Animism dictates that everything, even dead things have a vital force. "Good" was anything that enhanced that force, while "bad" reduced it. There is even a vague notion of a god who exists perpetually just out of reach.

A charming story…but one that leaves Africans trapped in darkness.

When we returned to the States, a group of us began to film speaking engagements of various Christian intellectuals. We put them on cable access in several states. One of these events celebrated Earth Day. It featured several prominent scientists, including one who had signed the original Earth Day document.

At this weeklong event, we heard from Stephen Bouma-Prediger, the Jacobson professor of Religion at Hope College. He had authored a book discussing Christianity and ecology entitled *For the Beauty of the Earth.*

His book was a response to those who blame pollution on Christians. That list is lengthy and includes notables like Arnold Toynbee (historian) as well as more familiar names like the Sierra Club. Their rational: as dualists (believing in both soul and body) Christians see no value in protecting the environment, because only the soul is eternal. Their argument goes like this:

- Christians believe in both a physical body and a non-material soul.
- When we die, Christians believe the body returns to dust, but the soul, being eternal, does not.
- Christians are also taught that, one day, the earth would be burned up.
- The only possible conclusion for Christians is that while our soul is critical, the earth is expendable.
- Consequently, Christians believe there is no value in preserving our environment.

Do Christians cause pollution? Dr. Bouma-Prediger says "no." But it's why he says no that is troubling. They're wrong, he says, because they misunderstand Christianity's teaching about the soul. The truth, he explains, is that Christians do believe in a soul...just not one that is separate from our body.

Not separate from the body?

Yep, for Bouma-Prediger, "soul" is just another way of saying "dirt that's alive." [lxxxviii] He cites Genesis 2:7, which says: "Then the LORD God formed man of dust from the ground, and breathed into his nostrils the breath of life; and man became a living soul."

Quoting Wendell Berry, Bouma-Prediger explains:

The formula given in Genesis 2:7 is not man = body+soul; the formula there is soul=dust +breath. According to this verse, God did not make a body and put a soul into it, like a letter into an envelope. He formed man of dust; then, by breathing His breath into it, He made the dust live. The dust, formed as man and made to live, did not embody a soul; it became a soul. "Soul" here refers to the whole creature. Humanity is thus presented to us, in Adam, not as a creature of two discrete parts temporarily glued together but as a single mystery. [lxxxix]

Do you get it? Bouma-Prediger thinks humans have just one part, not two. And that one part is the dirt, or more accurately, "living" dirt. Even the name of the first man, 'Adam shares a similar root to the Hebrew 'Adamah, meaning "earth substance." So it's not surprising when Bouma-Prediger claims our first job description as little pieces of "living dirt" was to "protect" and "serve" the garden, a larger piece of dirt (Genesis 2:15). [xc]

We all know what happens next. Adam and Eve defy God and are evicted from the garden. Bouma-Prediger claims that mankind was no longer in charge. [xci xcii] And after the flood, a new contract is drawn up (Noahic), this time between God and ALL the animals (Genesis 9:9-17). [xciii] Bouma-Prediger explains that now the animals are our sisters and our brothers. [xciv] It's not clear if mankind is still considered special or just one of the gang. Bouma-Prediger says both. [xcv xcvi]

But for Bouma-Prediger, it's a happy ending because God promises that the earth will never again be destroyed. [xcvii xcviii] Instead it will be renewed by animal rights, biocentrism, the wilderness movement, land ethic, and deep ecology. [xcix] Along the way, sin, salvation, Jesus, and the Holy Spirit all are given new identities in relation to the earth.

[79]

Okay, so maybe this all sounds a little weird and perhaps you're thinking Bouma-Prediger's a one-off. After all, you've never heard of him before and you're not even sure where Hope College is. Not so fast.

Bouma-Prediger's book was endorsed by then president of the second largest evangelical seminary in America. ^c *Christianity Today* also jumped on board, praising Bouma-Prediger's ideas. A conference at Princeton, including many mainline churches, had several presenters who shared his perspective. And years ago, even the devotional, *Our Daily Bread*, alarmed at this heresy, made reference to this controversy.

But Dr. Bouma-Prediger isn't satisfied simply claiming that the soul is a piece of dirt that's been brought to life. Again quoting Berry, he adds: "The emphasis within the Christian tradition on dualisms of soul and body, spirit and matter, denigrate the earth and sanctions its misuse and exploitation" (Bouma-Prediger 66).[ci]

No dualisms. No "soul and body"…no "spirit and matter." That's because for Bouma-Prediger, there can only be "living dirt." Anything beyond that, such as a soul or spirit separate from the physical body, is too much.

And with that tiny change Bouma-Prediger moves into "spirit of the anti-Christ" territory.[cii]

Whoa…back the bus up, buddy. Where did that come from?

Answer: take a look at 1 John 4:1-3, a passage originally written to refute Gnosticism but also relevant here.

> "Beloved, do not believe every spirit, but test the spirits to see whether they are from God, because many false prophets have gone out into the world. By this you know the Spirit of God: every spirit that confesses that Jesus Christ has come in the flesh is from God; and every spirit that does not confess Jesus is not from God; this is the spirit of the antichrist, of which you have heard that it is coming, and now it is already in the world."

Okay, let me lay it out. Prior to the incarnation Jesus was spirit. But verse two says Jesus came in the flesh. So that means that Jesus was both spirit and body. That's one (spirit) plus one (body) equals two, also called dualism.

But Bouma-Prediger says there is no soul or spirit separate from the body. He counts only to one (also called non-dualism). But if you can only count to one then you cannot say that Jesus (spirit) came in the flesh (body). Or in the words of 1 John 4:3, "this is the spirit of the anti-christ."

So why or how did Dr. Bouma-Prediger get himself stuck in this quagmire?[ciii] I asked him via a letter. Initially he responded to me…then silence.

But two things are certain. First, he uses mistaken assumptions. And second, he quotes only verses which support his claims.

Unproven Assumptions (one example):

Dr. Bouma-Prediger opens his book with a quotation from Thomas Aquinas: "Any error about creation leads to an error about God."

Very witty. But ask yourself, is God diminished if we get the forecast wrong? Or if we can't measure a dog's tail right? Ditto, a thousand other exceptions. Over and over we have to qualify this claim to avoid saying something untrue. Ultimately we have to agree that this quote should "die the death of a thousand qualifications.".

But what if we insisted that even 10 million qualifications don't void the quotation from Aquinas? Well, if the Aquinas contention was correct, then God would be slandered every time we mess up the environment. Moreover, if we really want to know God, we would have to really know the environment. Either way, the stakes couldn't be higher. We would have to be sure. At the minimum we would need an environmental expert (ecologist) to be our guide.

And what would happen if you disagreed with Bouma-Prediger or his experts? You would be held in contempt and considered ignorant not just of the environment but also the very nature of God. Am I exaggerating? Read his book.

Selective Verses

Dr. Bouma-Prediger claims that "biblical texts—from Genesis to Revelation—and many basic Christian doctrines derived from the Bible" confirm his views. Really? If that's so then why doesn't he tell us what they are? We certainly don't see it in Chapter Four of his book, which has the ironic title, "What is the Connection between Scripture and Ecology"?

Regardless, it appears that the lynchpin of his argument is Genesis 2:7. That being so, his argument rises or falls on the claim that Adam is just a piece of dirt that God breathed on.

But just what does Bouma-Prediger mean by "dust plus breath"? He doesn't tell us. Instead we are left with a vision of God doing CPR on some man-shaped dirt, causing it to live.

Come on, the Bible has over 30,000 verses. Couldn't Bouma-Prediger find something in them to make sense of Genesis 2:7?

No? Well, I did. Let's look at Isaiah 42:5: "…Who spread out the earth and its offspring, Who gives breath (*neshamah*) to the people on it and spirit (*ruwach*)[civ] to those who walk in it." Further, Ezekiel 37:6, 10 says: "Behold I will cause spirit (*ruwach*) to enter you that you may come to life."

Both these verses describe a spirit (*ruwach*) which appears necessary for life. But Bouma-Prediger claims that we're just "living dirt" plus nothing else. The only time that Bouma-Prediger says anything about a spirit is to blame it for pollution.

> "The emphasis within the Christian tradition on dualisms of soul and body, **spirit and matter**, denigrate the earth and sanctions its misuse and exploitation" (Bouma-Prediger 71; bold emphasis mine).

And what about when we die? Does Bouma-Prediger think the dirt becomes unbreathed or maybe just less animated? The body's still there…even when it begins to decay. Can Bouma-Prediger explain why?[cv]

[82]

As Genesis 7:22 says: "Of all that was on the dry land, all in whose nostrils was the breath (*neshamah*) of the spirit (*ruwach*) of life, died" (written by Moses).

Moreover, Ecclesiastes 12:7 says: "Then the dust (`aphar)[cvi] will return to the earth as it was, and the spirit (*ruwach*) will return to God who gave it" (written by Solomon). This is seen again in Psalms 146:4 His spirit (*ruwach*) departs, he returns to the earth; In that very day his thoughts perish.

The Bible teaches that when we die the dust returns to the earth. And that's why it begins to decay. But there's also something that isn't dust. Moses, David, and Solomon all identify it as a spirit. Solomon explains that after death this "spirit" returns to God. Not one of them accept Dr. Bouma-Prediger's "living dirt" plus nothing else theory.

The Bible has over a dozen other verses like this. And I don't think Bouma-Prediger will be able to explain them either.

Human Nature and the Environment

So what does all this say about the soul? And how do those changes affect the environment?

From our previous discussion we know that spirit (*ruwach*) is necessary for the flesh to be alive. Mathematically that means that the soul has to be more than just one part, i.e. dust which has been animated. Now the dust (`aphar) includes not just the "breath of life" (*neshamah*) but also a spirit (*ruwach*).

But doesn't that put Christians right back in the crosshairs of those who denounce us as polluters? As I consider their accusations, I wonder how anyone could be so silly. Sadly, my experience says otherwise. A doctor friend, one who measures his worth by the trees he plants, called me a liar when I casually mentioned the 16,500 trees my brother and I had planted on my dad's farm in Shakopee, Minnesota. Apparently, for him at least, only people who shared his radical eco-centric vision did such things.

So what do we say to such people? Let's examine their argument.

They claim that as dualists, Christians see no value in protecting the environment because only the spirit and soul are eternal. Or as Prediger's book, *The Beauty of the Earth* succinctly explains: dualism "denigrates the earth and sanctions its misuse and exploitation." [cvii]

Mankind's call to stewardship of the earth

We've seen how Dr. Bouma-Prediger's first attempt to counter the pollution accusation ended up doing damage to God's word. But he has a second argument, one based upon Adam's job description in the Garden of Eden. Bouma-Prediger claims that Adam was never supposed to rule the garden, but serve it: "Then the LORD God took the man and put him into the garden of Eden to cultivate it and keep it" (Genesis 2:15).

Strong's concordance does say that `abad and *shamar*, translated "cultivate" and "keep" (NAS) can also be translated as "serve" and "protect." The garden is the priority; man is just a caretaker.

But the linguist reviewing my use of Hebrew and Greek has a problem with Dr. Bouma-Prediger's claims. He says:

> *Abad* certainly can mean 'serve,' as in Gen. 29:25, 27; 1 Sam. 4:9; and 2 Sam. 16:19. But I am unaware of any place where this happens when it refers to serving something that is non-personal, such as the land. Similar usages always mean 'till' or 'cultivate' (Gen. 4:2, 12; 2 Sam. 9:10; Zech 13:5; Isa. 30:24).

`Abad and *shamar* turn out to mean "cultivate and keep" the garden, not "protect and serve" as Dr. Bouma-Prediger claimed. But shouldn't Dr. Bouma-Prediger have suspected this already from God's declaration in Genesis 1:26 (repeated in 1:28)? It says: "God blessed them; and God said to them, 'be fruitful and multiply, and fill the earth, and subdue it; and rule over the fish of the sea and over the birds of the sky and over every living thing that moves on the earth.'"

Adam is to subdue the earth and rule over it. But Adam is still just God's steward, not the Master. And that stewardship comes with accountability.[cviii]

[84]

To understand exactly what that means, consider Luke 12:48, a passage on stewardship: "From everyone who has been given much, much will be required; and to whom they entrusted much, of him they will ask all the more."

So how can we know if we're doing it right, you know, being a good steward? That's easy, we can look at how God does it.

God cares for His creation. He waters the mountains, causes the earth to be fruitful, provides tall trees and food for the birds, beauty for the lilies, food for the wild donkeys, feed for cattle, prey for the lions, mountains for the goats, cliffs for the *shephanim*, and waters for fish, both great and small. He even guides the sun and provides the moon for seasons (Matthew 6:26-29, Psalm 104, Matthew 10:29).

And God honors His creation. He uses animals to teach us right behavior, to acknowledge a job well done, and even to define His own character.

Showing right behavior:

(Wisdom for successful living): "Go to the ant, O sluggard, Observe her ways and be wise" (Proverbs 6:6).

(Obedience): "Know that the LORD Himself is God; It is He who has made us, and not we ourselves; We are His people and the sheep of His pasture" (Psalm 100:3).

(Clever Awareness): "Behold, I send you out as sheep in the midst of wolves; so be shrewd as serpents and innocent as doves" (Matthew 10:16).

(Safe Harbor): "I am the good shepherd; the good shepherd lays down His life for the sheep" (John 10:11).

(Hearing and Obeying God's Heart) "My sheep hear My voice, and I know them, and they follow Me" (John 10:27).

This continues as God compares the best of us to His creation.

A job well done:

(Bravery) "And even the one who is valiant, whose heart is like the heart of a lion" (2 Samuel 17:10).

(Renewal) "Who satisfies your years with good things, So that your youth is renewed like the eagle" (Psalm 103:5).

(Boldness) "But the righteous are bold as a lion" (Proverbs 28:1).

To reveal His character:

The Bible, at times, even compares God and Jesus to His creation:

(God's voice) "A lion has roared! Who will not fear? The Lord GOD has spoken! Who can but prophesy?" (Amos 3:8).

(Humility of Christ) "Rejoice greatly, O daughter of Zion! Shout in triumph, O daughter of Jerusalem! Behold, your king is coming to you; He is just and endowed with salvation, humble, and mounted on a donkey, even on a colt, the foal of a donkey" (Zechariah 9:9).

(Christ and His Church) "Let us rejoice and be glad and give the glory to Him, for the marriage of the Lamb has come and His bride has made herself ready" (Revelation 19:7).

(God as protector) "Enfolding us with His wing He will cover you with His pinions, and under His wings you may seek refuge" (Psalm 91:4).

Specific instructions

The Bible also gives us specific instructions to help us to steward God's creation. These include acknowledging the partnerships between ourselves and His creation as well as specific instructions for that care: "For every species of beasts and birds, of reptiles and creatures of the sea, is tamed and has been tamed by the human race" (James 3:7).

But this partnership comes with rules:

[86]

Partners between humanity and animals

(Stewardship of ownership) "Know well the condition of your flocks, and pay attention to your herds" (Proverbs 27:23).

(Stewardship implied even without ownership) "You shall not see your countryman's ox or his sheep straying away, and pay no attention to them; you shall certainly bring them back to your countryman" (Deuteronomy 25:1).

(Stewardship of animal suffering) "A righteous man has regard for the life of his animal, but even the compassion of the wicked is cruel" (Proverbs 12:10).

(Stewardship of animal health) "Donkeys rest '…on the seventh day…you shall cease from labor so that your ox and your donkey may rest...may refresh themselves'" (Proverbs 27:23).

(Stewardship of animal rights) "You shall not muzzle the ox while he is threshing" (Deuteronomy 25:4).

(Stewardship of animal care and biblical law) "And He said to them, 'What man is there among you who has a sheep, and if it falls into a pit on the Sabbath, will he not take hold of it and lift it out?" (Matthew 12:11)

Partnership with the land

(Resting the land) "But on the seventh year you shall let it rest and lie fallow, so that the needy of your people may eat" (Exodus 23:11a).

(Resting the vineyard every 7 years) "You are to do the same with your vineyard" (Exodus 23:11b).

(Not maliciously assaulting nature) "When you besiege a city a long time, to make war against it in order to capture it, you shall not destroy its trees by swinging an axe against them; for you may eat from them, and you shall not cut them down. For is the tree of the field a man, that it should be besieged by you?"

[87]

(Deuteronomy 20:19).

(Stewardship of necessity, only cutting at time of need) "Only the trees which you know are not fruit trees you shall destroy and cut down, that you may construct siegeworks against the city that is making war with you until it falls" (Deuteronomy 20:20).

Okay, fine, but doesn't mankind's stewardship go away after the flood? No, it is actually expanded to include all the animals in addition to green plants.

The fear of you and the terror of you will be on every beast of the earth and on every bird of the sky; with everything that creeps on the ground, and all the fish of the sea, into your hand they are given. Every moving thing that is alive shall be food for you; I give all to you, as I gave the green plant. (Genesis 9:2-3)

The word translated "gave (to you)" is from the Hebrew "*nathan.*" The idea is "given under one's authority." [cix] This verse has a triple declaration.

- Animals will fear us.
- Animals are food for us.
- Animals are entrusted to us, once again as stewards, making us accountable for their treatment.

So we need to look carefully at the context to appreciate what God is saying: "I give all to you, as I gave the green plant."

Do you recognize the simile, introduced by the preposition "as?" Recall that similes use like/as to compare two different things to give us a brand new meaning.

God first lists all living animals. Then a simile is used to illustrate the manner that God gives them to mankind. The giving will be as it was for the plants. This means that the manner in which man was given the plants would be applied to the animals. And what manner was that? To get that answer we have to go back to Genesis Chapters One and Two.

Unquestionably green plants are given for food (Genesis 1:29). That is obviously a proper meaning in this passage. But green plants are

[88]

also to be cared for by man, God's steward: "Now no shrub of the field was yet in the earth, and no plant of the field had yet sprouted, for the LORD God had not sent rain upon the earth, and there was no man to cultivate the ground" (Genesis 2:5).

Both before and after the flood man is entrusted to be God's steward of the plants and animals. Mankind was to rule over God's creation, acting as stewards who are accountable to God.

Conclusion

The Bible gives us an exalted view of our world. Both pre- and post-diluvian (flood) humanity was entrusted with the stewardship of God's creation, the earth. Historically there are many times when we abused this charter. Certainly all creation presently groans under the weight of our sin (Romans 8:22). But Dr. Bouma-Prediger's distortions have been hurtful, not helpful. Perhaps he (or others) will be moved to a proper study of God's word on His works and our stewardship as citizens in this world. But that study should begin with a correct understanding of God's exalted view of humanity made with both body and spirit. It cannot be repeated enough: "He jealously desires the Spirit which He has made to dwell in us" (James 4:5).

1 + 1 = 2. Isn't it grand?

SIX

Minding the Brain

"At the head of the noisy streets" (a confusion of voices)

Proverbs 1:21a

Carved into the mountainside, the road was barely adequate and he'd been going too fast. The Tutsi kid tried to brake, but his piki[cx] just slid on the volcanic scree. In moments he was airborne, eerily catapulting over thick brush and terraced gardens, inevitably careening into the sharp rocks below, his fall broken by thick banana trees.

When I saw him he was still covered with sticks and leaves. His arms and legs lay motionless. Terrified, his large brown eyes locked onto mine, pleading for anything. An older sibling wiped blood from his brother's face.

A brief exam confirmed the paralysis…just a flicker of movement at his shoulders. I applied traction, and then took an X-ray of his neck. Water dripped off the fresh x-ray onto the floor as I did a "wet" reading. There was no fracture. I held it up in the African sun…nothing. I repeated my exam. The ligaments were stable. I had no explanation for his paralysis.

I was a brand-new doc. As I re-checked the traction, I prayed for help. But from where? We were remote; minutes from where Dian Fossey had studied the mountain guerillas. A tribe of cannibals lived just to our north. This was the deep jungle.

Four days later, a Rover stopped at the front of the hospital. The driver had been visiting his daughter who worked across the border for the Peace Corps. He asked to join me on rounds. As the only doctor I welcomed an English-speaking companion.

As I led this man inside the hospital, he turned to me. "Oh, by the way," he said, "I'm a pediatric neurology professor from Harvard."

That'll do.[cxi]

****

We all need help. And I felt like that was true for my last chapter. It needed an addendum. Well, not so much an addendum as a look at the flip side of the (non-dualistic) coin.

On the first side we discussed Bouma-Prediger's spiritual non-dualism. But when we turn the coin over we discover scientific non-dualism, i.e. scientism. Historian Jacques Barzun defined this as "the fallacy [mistake] of believing...science...will settle every issue."

By the way, these beliefs are all over the place. They're in your kid's school. They're in our culture and entertainment. They may even be in your church.

So let's begin by asking scientism the same things we asked Bouma-Prediger. The questions are going to look a little different because of the initial assumptions. With scientism we're going to look at the mind/brain question.

Okay...I agree. This is a sleepy topic. But you'd better wake up for two reasons. First, for Christians, the mind/brain question is really the soul/brain controversy.[cxii] And second, it's one of the biggies Satan is already using to mess with your kids' faith.

So cutting to the chase, our question really asks if we're robots or whether we have a soul with free will. Has the universe pre-programmed you to brush your teeth each morning...or do you decide what you do? Just so you know, at this time, the first option (robots) is held by a large number of philosophers and psychologists in America.

The robot argument claims we have no mind. There's only a brain. Once again, for you Christians that means just a physical brain and no soul. These philosophers claim that everything that happens…whether you marvel at the sunset or feel your pulse quicken as you fall in love…is just chemicals mixing together. For them, believing that the sun's beauty explains your admiration…or falling in love explains your swooning heart…would just be a "category error." That's the term Gilbert Ryle introduced to refute those who argue for the mind by listing activities of the brain. Ryle insists that all the activities of the brain can be explained chemically. Ryle also claimed that wrongly attaching things of one kind (feelings of awe) to another (an actual experience of beauty) was like saying you came in a taxi and left in a rage. For Ryle, and those like him…there's only the brain.

But people like Ryle have a problem that refuses to go away. Hollywood knows what it is and has used it non-stop to create ridiculous horror films. It's called "self-awareness" and it's especially creepy when non-human things like houses and lawn mowers (e.g. Maximum Overdrive)…or even robots possess it. That's because human characteristics are unsettling when they are expressed by things or machines.

But in humans, "self-awareness" is natural, the crowning mark of our humanity. Self-awareness is the idea that we know that we know. Think back to high school when you spoke to that cute girl or boy. Even as you declared your feelings you were listening in and grading your effort. That "self-awareness" is also called consciousness. And Robert Doty claims that it "remains the cardinal mystery of human existence."

UCLA neuropsychiatrist Jeff Schwartz tracks our current academic confusion between the mind and brain to the 17th century French philosopher Rene Descartes. Descartes was a brilliant mathematician and even tutored the Queen of Sweden. But his real passion was to discover how we know that we know.

To answer this, Descartes divided reality into two categories: 1) the mind (*res cogitans*) and 2) the world, including the physical brain (*res extensa*). He couldn't have anticipated the disastrous consequences of this simple idea.

Descartes started by asking what he could trust for certain. Definitely not the physical world; perhaps he was just in a dream existing in a fantasy world. Nor could he trust his senses. A straight stick looks bent in water; a lump of wax appears to be solid until put near a flame.

Ultimately Descartes decided that the only thing he could trust was his own mind, the fact that he was really thinking. Ironically, even doubting that he was thinking was still a thought.

But a bigger problem remained. Descartes couldn't explain how a non-physical mind could be connected to the physical brain (or to the rest of the body).[cxiii]

Okay, this mind-brain stuff is weird. It should be, right? It has to do with us, and we humans are peculiar creatures. Especially when we're doing the investigating and we're also under the microscope. So I wanted to give you an example that would help ease your headache. I'm gonna take you to school. Don't worry. Just to kindergarten.

What do I mean? Well, a little show-and-tell. Remember when you used to scrounge around last minute for an "interesting" object? I got one for you, from my friend Wittgenstein.[cxiv] A beetle in a box.

Huh? Well, you see, the beetle in a box gives us a chance to think about how we have a mind, and how strange it is that the mind and brain get along and work as a team.

So, show and tell. Bring your beetle to the front of the class. Hold it up. Smile! But hang on. What's with the box, someone says. Why can't you open it up?

Well, you would. But…there's a problem. The box you're holding…is your brain. Gross, right? It's wooden, nobody can see through it. And you can't take the cover off. The beetle would get away. Oh, the beetle…that's your mind.

So there you are, telling everyone about how amazing the beetle is, while their eyes glaze over. You shake the box. How could they not believe you? You really do have a beetle! Your teacher rubs her temples and says, "Next time bring your grandpa."

[93]

So is this a mind trip yet? How exciting could the brain be if it was just an empty box? Could it do anything? How weird is it that no one but ourselves can see our beetle (through self-consciousness). What a trip, the entire human race, a bunch of magnificent boxes and beetles!

Well, you can probably see why some scientists, like your bored classmates, leave the beetle behind. Working with a beetle-in-the-box hypothesis violates the scientific dogma that every claim must be proven scientifically. That's why these scientists are so comfortable with giving the mind/soul and all the unprovable stuff to the Church while keeping the real stuff (i.e. brain) for themselves.

Moreover, they are increasingly emboldened to teach your kids that the mind/soul is just a myth. This academic condescension is reflected by the recent European declaration for 2014 to be the "year of the brain." A year earlier in America, over a hundred million dollars was directed into mapping the brain, with the goal of forever extinguishing the notion of a soul. For many academics, the concept of the mind is an embarrassment; one which neuroscientist Steven Rose says needs to go away. Dr. Jeff Schwartz records no less than ten separate attempts to accomplish this, including David Chalmers' "don't have a clue materialism."[cxv]

Enter PET scans and functional MRI's. Once used by neuroscientists to crush the concept of mind, Dr. Schwartz now uses them to accomplish the opposite. His book, *The Mind and the Brain* is, in Dr. Floyd Bloom's opinion,[cxvi] both profound and engaging. Skipping ahead, Dr. Schwartz proposes that the mind rewires the brain using "mental force." Dr. Schwartz's claim has now been confirmed after testing with EEG's and PET scans.

Simply put, the mind (or soul for Christians) has been proven to program the brain.

Okay, this next part is a little dry. But I promise that if you work your way through it I am going to show you an amazing confirmation of God's word.

****

[94]

Dr. Schwartz first challenged the canon that said that the non-physical mind couldn't be studied scientifically. He already knew from the Silver Springs monkey experiments that the brain could, in fact, be rewired. The VA has already used the Silver Springs research clinically with patients to rewire the brains of stroke victims. Other researchers have helped musicians rewire their brains to correct their dystonia (two fingers moving as one). Still others have proved that rewiring of the brain could be done with simple contemplation. In one particularly stunning case, a patient with locked in syndrome was taught to rewire his brain to move a computer cursor.

Dr. Schwartz has done extensive work on broken brain circuits found in patients with obsessive compulsive disorder (OCD). His group at UCLA was the first to verify the power of free will to rewire these abnormal OCD circuits with healthier circuits. This work has been confirmed both clinically and with PET scans proving the power of the mind to physically re-wire the brain in mental activity. Let me say that once again. Dr. Schwartz has confirmed the power of the (non-physical) mind to re-wire the physical, thinking part of the brain.

Dr. Schwartz also studied the power of the mind to physically re-wire the brain with habitual muscle movement. Dr. Schwartz recounted Ben Libet's work revealing a 350 milliseconds delay between brain waves and conscious awareness of muscle movement. In mental thought 350 milliseconds is an eternity leaving the mind plenty of time to allow or block the activity. Further studies confirmed Schwartz's discovery, showing that participants could decide whether or not routine activities would be allowed, i.e. whether they would take another step while walking down the street. Dr. Schwartz has called the power of the mind to block the brain with habitual behavior a kind of "free won't." Ben Libet's work confirms the power of the (non-physical) mind to re-wire the behavioral part of the physical brain.

What this means is that something that is non-material, i.e. mind/soul is able to re-wire the brain in both mental (thinking) and physical activity ("free won't").

****

To some, the idea of free will is elusive, a metaphor. But in a thought experiment, Dr. Schwartz correctly concluded that if we really were robots, we could never be ethically wrong. That's because we'd be like machines, and machines don't make moral choices. You might kick a vending machine if it doesn't dispense your Coke, but you wouldn't argue with it.

But according to materialists, people are robots. Or said more bluntly, they don't have "free will." But no "free will" means that that we are just machines and it is impossible for machines to sin. So nothing immoral was ever done when 6 million Jews were killed by Hitler. Someone should tell that to the survivors.[cxvii]

In Genesis 2:7 we discover that our humanity, the thing that separates us from robots, began on Day Six when we became a "living soul": "Then the Lord God formed man of dust from the ground, and breathed into his nostrils the breath of life; and man became a living soul [*nephesh*]."

This Hebrew word *nephesh* includes mind, desire, emotion, passion, appetites, and character. Our flesh became a living soul. We're not robots. We think, we desire, we have emotions.

And we choose freely. God's word tells us we have free will, that is, the opportunity to choose. And those choices necessarily depend upon our motives, which may be good or bad (Proverbs 16:2).

Said bluntly, no choice means no sin, because sin requires free-will. That we freely choose is supported by PET scans. And the consequences of those choices, whether good or bad, are a logical outcome.

Dr. Schwartz has assembled a four-part sequence which he teaches as he helps people use their minds to overwrite their brains. The individual steps include:

> **1) Relabeling:** identifying the feeling/urge accompanying the obsessive behavior as a false message
> **2) Reattributing:** assigning the false message to a brain disease and not the person himself

3) Refocusing: redirecting the attention into some adaptive behavior
4) Revaluing: giving wise attention to see matters in accordance with the truth

Relabeling clarifies what's happening. Obsessive urges are false message from the brain.

Reattributing clarifies why they happen. These obsessive urges are from pathologic circuits.

Refocusing is when the mind redirects the brain from a "bad" habitual circuit to a "good" habitual circuit.

Revaluing is a process of wise attention to truth. It's really a discipline of practicing the first three steps until quantumly these new circuits outnumber the damaged circuits which are being pruned away.

As I read through Dr. Schwartz' research I was struck by its similarity to 2 Timothy 3:16-17: "All Scripture is inspired by God and profitable for teaching, for reproof, for correction, for training in righteousness; so that the man of God may be adequate, equipped for every good work."

The four parts in these two verses run parallel (with notable differences) to the steps described by Dr. Schwartz that the mind uses to rewire the brain.

The Brain	The Spirit
Relabeling	Doctrine/Teaching
Reattributing	Reproof/Prove absolutely wrong
Refocusing	Correction
Revaluing	Training in Righteousness

We learn from 2 Timothy 3:16 that "teaching" means showing us God's absolute standard. It comes from the Greek *didaskalia*, which means doctrine. Doctrine, another "churchy" word literally means practical concepts in living…in this case, doctrine flowing out of God's

[97]

mind.

Dr. Schwartz' first step of "relabeling" gives a new perspective to patients with abnormal OCD circuits. *Didaskalia* gives us a new perspective of our sinful practices by comparing them to God's holy standard.[cxviii]

Dr. Schwartz' second step is one of "reattributing." In this case "reattribution" means that the patient reassigns any false message to a damaged circuit in his brain and not himself personally. The Christian's second step, "reproof," is also a "reattribution."[cxix] For Christians, reattribution means that we stop attributing (blaming) our behavior to others or society. We instead "re-attribute" the behavior to ourselves. From Dr. Schwartz' Buddhist perspective, we would take ownership of our Karma. For the Christian this means we plead guilty to violating God's standard, we confess. Confession, from the Greek *exomologeo*, literally means to say the same thing as, to agree. The Christian agrees with God that his behavior is not simply wrong or unfortunate or untimely. It's sin.

Dr. Schwartz' third step is refocusing. The patient redirects his/her attention into some adaptive behavior. The Christian's third step is also a refocusing, or correction (*epanorthosis*).[cxx] This word means "to correct" our old practices by choosing godly behavior.[cxxi]

This brings us to Dr. Schwarz' last and probably most important step. In this step the patient is asked to revalue matters as they really are. He explains this means giving wise attention in accordance with the truth. It is also the most critical step for the Christian. The Bible claims to give us **"training** in righteousness" (bold emphasis mine).[cxxii] This means that we adopt a discipline to practice steps one through three aligning with God's truth until they become habitual.

The concept is one of change, becoming something else...like the not-so-funny joke: when is a door not a door? The not-so-funny answer: when it's a jar. The same is true of us. When are we no longer a slave to some behavior? Answer: when we become something else.

This is totally compatible with the "put off's" and "put on's" of Ephesians Chapter Four. Verse 28 says: "He who steals must steal no longer; but rather he must labor, performing with his own hands what is good, so that he will have something to share with one who has need."

When is a thief not a thief? When he stops stealing? No, he's just between jobs. He has to finish the third step.

He has already put off, "stealing no longer." But then he puts on, laboring, producing goods, sharing with those in need. The Bible is actually full of these put off's and put on's. But to capture it all in one verse I went to 2 Corinthians 5:17: "Therefore if anyone is in Christ, he is a new creature; the old things passed away; behold, new things have come."

2 Timothy 3:17 explains that practicing right behavior is a discipline. Hebrews 5:14 adds: "But solid food is for the mature, who because of practice have their senses trained to discern good and evil."

An important caveat as I conclude. Whenever one writes something, one runs the risk of unscrupulous persons taking this material and changing it into what it is not. What I have written does not say that Dr. Schwartz' four steps are the same as 2 Timothy 3:16-17. It does, however, say that his research corroborates each of the truth claims found in these verses.

The steps found in 2 Timothy 3:16-17 are not just some kind of feel-good spiritualism. They represent a path we can walk using God's rules to become like Christ.

In summary, we find that the Bible solves the challenges of the mind/brain controversy, fitting the science of a changing brain, using the mind (soul) to rewrite the brain producing quantum expectation of new behaviors.

Fitting the science exactly.

SEVEN

Hope and Change

"At the entrance of the gates in the city" (politics of change).

Proverbs 1:21b

I always saw them first. These were the really sick…found in front of the hospital on make-shift litters, brought in at first light…the equivalent of an African ambulance.

The closest one did not stir. He was almost dead when I saw him. I examined him quickly. His posturing and his eyes told the whole story. He was herniating his brain. He'd be dead in minutes.

Our remote hospital in the Ruwenzori's of Africa had no oxygen and very little IV fluid (we made our own from the river), let alone CAT scans. But his mother brought him anyway.

HOPE.

He'd fallen out of a tree and now he was dying. I couldn't hurt him. In my first year of residency we'd been trained in burr holes, but this hospital had no equipment. So I drilled his head with a borrowed Black and Decker drill. You can't imagine my relief as dark non-clotting blood poured out.

A day later he woke up. The next day he moved. Two more and he began to speak. On the third day he walked away from the hospital.

CHANGE.

****

In the last two elections we heard a lot about "hope and change."[cxxiii] From our innermost fiber we are like that mother. We know something's broken. It makes sense to want it fixed.

Years before the presidential election these same words were powerfully spoken by the political genius, Saul Alinsky, considered the founder of modern community activism. Our president, working as activist in several Alinsky projects, shared similar goals and tactics.

Truthfully, I'd never thought very deeply about Alinsky until my son, Caleb began to do some freelance research on this matter. I was struck by Alinsky's pithy position statement "peace, justice, and equality." I'd heard that once before…but phrased a little differently.

So I read a couple of Alinsky's books. And I found the complete version of Alinsky's position statement:

> [W]e are concerned with how to create mass organizations to seize power and give it to the people; to realize the democratic dream of equality, justice, peace, cooperation, equal and full opportunities for education, full and useful employment, health, and the creation of those circumstances in which men have the chance to live by the values that give meaning to life. We are talking about a mass power organization which will change the world…This means revolution.

I count nine goals. The last election introduced many of them into our daily conversation. To a Christian, they sound attractive, almost spiritual.

But that's probably because they are. That is, they address the same spiritual issues addressed by Proverbs...which is where I first heard the altered position statement, "righteousness, justice, and equity."

Next, I looked at the expanded position statement from Proverbs, chapter one. And <u>eight of Alinsky's nine goals clash violently with God's truths found in these verses</u>.

> "To know wisdom and instruction, to discern the sayings of understanding, to receive instruction in wise behavior, righteousness, justice and equity; to give prudence to the naive, to the youth knowledge and discretion [purpose], a wise man will hear and increase in learning, and a man of understanding will acquire wise counsel, to understand a proverb and a figure, the words of the wise and their riddles" (Proverbs 1:2-6).

Solomon	Alinsky
1. Righteousness	"Peace"
2. Justice	"Social justice"
3. Equity	"Democratic equality"
4. Wisdom/calling	Vocation
5. Prudence	"Cooperation"
6. Purpose	"Values"
7. Learning	"Education"
8. Wise counsel	"Organization"

To appreciate just how striking this is we are going to examine a number of these dualities.

Solomon's Righteousness and Alinsky's Peace

Let's begin with Solomon's righteousness.[cxxiv] [cxxv] Righteousness. Okay, so what's that got to do with Alinsky's peace? Once again, that is exactly the right question.

The answer is that "God's righteousness" is irrevocably tied to "peace." James 3:18 says: "And the seed whose fruit is righteousness is sown in peace by those who make peace." Psalms 85:10b adds: "Righteousness and peace have kissed each other" (Psalms 85:10b).

Finally, Isaiah 32:17 states: "...and the work of righteousness will be peace." cxxvi (Isaiah 32:17)

The simple truth is that biblical peace references the conflict between mankind and God. This conflict stems from man's rebellion against God, a rebellion which gives birth to conflict between people. The Bible explains that both conflicts are resolved by a substitutionary transfer of righteousness from Jesus. Ultimately that action leads to peace between ourselves and God: "Having been justified by faith, we have peace with God through our Lord Jesus Christ" (Romans 5:1).

We then become empowered to perform right thoughts and actions: "For we are His workmanship created in Christ Jesus for good works..." (Ephesians 2:10).

For the Christian, peace is something rooted in right thinking and behavior which pleases God. The first step is "peace with God." And that peace leads to peace with others: "When a man's ways are pleasing to the Lord, He makes even his enemies to be at peace with him" (Proverbs 16:7; see also Isaiah 59:8; Malachi 2:6).

Let me repeat that. Conflict between us and God brings conflict between us and others. Peace between us and God has the result of peace of bringing peace between us and others.

Compare this to Alinsky's peace. He claims that real peace can never happen without rebellion. Alinsky doesn't simply praise rebellion; he actually dedicates his book to Satan's rebellion from God.cxxvii

For Alinsky, the conflict isn't between God and man, but between those with wealth and those in poverty (the "haves" and the "have-nots"). In Alinsky's mind, the poor are not sinners. Instead they are innocent victims. Peace can only be accomplished by plundering one person's wealth and giving it to others, an action Alinsky justifies in the name of "fairness." Alinsky's "fairness" means replacing rules which protect freedom and property with a kind of mob rule: "They heal the brokenness of the daughter of My people superficially, saying, Peace, peace, But there is no peace" (Jeremiah 8:11).

[W]e are concerned," Alinsky elaborated, "with how to create mass organizations to seize power." To accomplish this they must take over institutions of power: the town councils, news media, boards of education, schools, universities, legislature, and presidencies.

To generate this "mass movement" Alinsky appeals to the public's greed and envy,[cxxviii] motives he renames "self-interest." But Alinsky sees neither greed nor envy as the problem. These are only step-children created by the real conflict, that of economic inequality. For Alinsky, the only restoration ever necessary is economic.[cxxix]

Alinsky's Social Justice and Solomon's Justice

In *Reveille for Radicals*, Alinsky describes a union boss telling this activist that "stealing" can be good if it makes it fair.

"Fairness." It reminds me of a question an African nurse once asked about the AIDS epidemic in her country.

Nurse: "What's going to happen?

Myself: "People have to change…or they'll die.

Nurse: "That's not fair…just 'cause our women are so generous."

That country now has the highest HIV rate in the world.

"Fairness" is also promoted by Alinsky. And just like the African nurse, "fairness" means anything he wants it to be. For him, that means whatever moves his agenda forward.

To accomplish this, Alinsky uses words as weapons, twisted to the point of non-recognizability.

…He says that he is not bound to traditional codes…then produces one as old as Rome.

…He claims he has no ideology; then produces an ideology.

…He claims he has no set principles, then describes dogma after dogma. Marxists venerate this manipulation of language as meanings are equivocated, inverted, conflated, and obscured.

...He likens the "common good" with the greatest "personal value." But "the common good" is just a euphemism for the good of the State. It is not a person, nor is it personal. Your value is determined by your value to the State. Permitting Alinsky to mangle truth like this allows him to plunder real "persons" to promote his impersonal State.

...He extols human freedom, but then steals our freedoms to control the environment, energy, and wealth.

...He endorses local governing which he then admits he uses as a puppet to push his agenda.

...He calls for universal education, but condemns any teaching which is not State controlled.

...He admits his "inconsistency" but claims this confirms he is consistent.

...He says man is rewarded by labor; but redirects the goods produced to the state, forbidding any privilege earned/given by this labor.

...He promotes inner dignity, but endorses violence when anyone's dignity disagrees with his agenda.

...He explains that brutality committed by the masses is justified and actually the fault of its victims.

...He endorses lying, manipulating, and basically anything necessary; the "ends justify the means."

...He believes that his vision is so good and so bright that it excuses every act of war.

For Alinsky, this is justice.

Solomon had something different in mind. Previously we considered 1 Kings 3 where Solomon is granted wisdom and understanding (*shema*). But to what end? The passage explains: "to bring justice (*mishpat*) to the nation."

Solomon could not have been unaware of the Great Commandment given by Moses from God in Deuteronomy 6:4. It begins: "*Shema*, Oh Israel." Hear oh Israel. It follows with an admonition to love God with all our heart, soul, strength, and mind. For Solomon, justice flows from God: "... He is a shield to those who walk in integrity, guarding the paths of justice, and He preserves the way of His godly ones." (Proverbs 2:7-8).

1 Kings 3 records the results of Solomon's petition for wisdom. Shortly after God gave Solomon wisdom, two women, both of poor reputation, presented their argument to the King. Each claimed the same newborn to be their own. Solomon called for a sword to divide the child in half. The real mother immediately relinquished her claim, for she loved the child. Solomon had discerned the truth. All of Israel watched in awe, "for they saw that the wisdom of God was in him to administer justice" (1 Kings 3:28, Psalm 37:30; 2 Chronicles 9:8).

Having looked at Biblical justice and Alinsky's "social justice" let's see what the Bible says about people like Alinsky.

Both Old and New Testament condemn Alinsky's use of greed and envy to motivate the people's plunder of another's property.

> "...[Greed and envy lead to the] wrath of God" (Colossians 3:5-6).

> "Woe to him...without righteousness...without justice, who uses his neighbor's services without pay..." (Jeremiah 22:13).

> "A wicked man receives a bribe from the bosom to pervert the ways of justice" (Proverbs 17:23).

Ezekiel renounces Alinsky's use of the state to enforce this plunder.

> "Enough, you princes of Israel....Stop your expropriations [plunder] from My people..." (Ezekiel 45:9).

Solomon exposes Alinsky's "common good," a noble lie created so that people will feel good about their felony. This lie claims that "state-sponsored theft" provides good will to everyone. In reality the "common good" is just a euphemism for the "state" and "state-sponsored theft."

> "A rascally witness makes a mockery of justice, and the mouth of the wicked spreads iniquity" (Proverbs 19:28).

Biblical justice condemns Alinsky's slander of opponents with whom (by his own admission) he has only trivial differences.

> "As for a rogue, his weapons are evil; He devises wicked schemes to destroy the afflicted with slander, even though the needy one speaks what is right" (Isaiah 32:7).

> "They speak mere words, with worthless oaths they make covenants; and judgment sprouts like poisonous weeds in the furrows of the field" (Hosea 10:4).

The Bible exposes Alinsky's provocation of the masses to follow him in "state-sponsored theft."

> "You shall not follow the masses in doing evil, nor shall you testify in a dispute so as to turn aside after a multitude in order to pervert justice" (Exodus 21:2).

> "An arrogant man stirs up strife, but he who trusts in the LORD will prosper" (Proverbs 28:25).

Solomon's justice terrorizes and threatens Alinsky as it exposes his true agenda.

> "The exercise of justice is joy for the righteous, but is terror to the workers of iniquity" (Proverbs 21:15).

The Bible condemns Alinsky's willingness to embrace brutality and violence to accomplish his plan.

> "Keep far from a false charge, and do not kill the innocent or the righteous, for I (God) will not acquit the guilty" (Exodus 23:7).

[107]

Biblical justice teaches that Alinsky's hatred of the wealthy is not enough to justify his barbary.

> "If you meet your enemy's ox or his donkey wandering away, you shall surely return it to him" (Exodus 23:5).

The Bible further rejects Alinsky's inconsistent standards, created to maintain an illusion of justice.

> "[There will be] one standard for the stranger as well as the native, for I am the LORD your God" (Lev 24:22; 25:18; Deut. 6:20; 30:16; 1 Chronicles 22:13).

Alinsky's "social justice" is called unjust, shameless, and perverted.

> "Therefore the law is ignored And justice is never upheld. For the wicked surround the righteous; Therefore justice comes out perverted" (Habakkuk 1:4).

The bottom line is that the Bible uses the strongest language to renounce Alinsky's justice.

> "You shall not be partial to the poor nor defer to the great, but you are to judge your neighbor fairly" (Leviticus 19:15; Ecclesiastes 5:8).

> "Nor shall you be partial to a poor man in his dispute" (Exodus 23:3).

> "You shall not show partiality in judgment; you shall hear the small and the great alike. You shall not fear man, for the judgment is God's" (Deuteronomy 1:17; Proverbs 18:5; Proverbs 24:23).

> "You shall not pervert the justice due to your needy brother in his dispute" (Exodus 23:6).

> "O LORD, do not Your eyes look for truth? Then I said, 'They are only the poor, they are foolish; For they do not know the way of the LORD or the ordinance of their God'" (Jeremiah 5:4).

[108]

This is not saying God's thrilled with what we've done with justice.

And one day, God plans to set everything right…to judge all lawbreakers.

> "Yet know that God will bring you to judgment for all these things [and to right all wrongs]" (Ecclesiastes 11:9b).

> "I will make justice the measuring line and righteousness the level..." (Isaiah 28:17).

But until that day, He wants us to use biblical justice to redeem our lives, our relationships, and our country. We should:

> "…Store up sound wisdom for the upright; He is a shield to those who walk in integrity, guarding the paths of justice" (Proverbs 2:7-8).

> "Learn to do good; seek justice, reprove the ruthless, defend the orphan, plead for the widow" (Isaiah 1:17).

> "Hate evil, love good, and establish justice in the gate [the place where judgments are made]!" (Amos 5:15).

> "…speak the truth to one another; judge with truth and judgment for peace in your gates" (Zechariah 8:16).

> "But to do justice, to love kindness, And to walk humbly with your God…" (Micah 6:8).

Alinsky's Equality and Solomon's Equity

Equality for Alinsky is a patchwork which, in his words, excludes a "materialistic society," "property rights," "conservatives," "privilege and power (inherited or acquired)," "haves," and capitalists. Moreover, it embraces both socialism and the "have-nots." Alinsky has no patience with liberals who are not true radicals. Alinsky blames capitalists for "unemployment," "decay," "disease," "crime," "distrust," "bigotry," "disorganization," and "demoralization."

[109]

Alinsky believes that since the roots cannot be isolated, <u>every "material or spiritual" root must be purged</u>. That includes our churches and our culture. Communities will be "manipulated" (Alinsky's word choice) by puppet leaders (i.e. educators, ministers, scientists) to line up with his agenda.

He does this by stirring up our natural resentments which puts him on the "side of the people." His enemy is demonized, even though the differences are often trivial.

The result? Equality is a scam. It's just a contrived value assigned to us by the state as we match Alinsky's socialist expectations.

Compare this to Biblical "equity." "Equity" is translated from the Hebrew word *meyshar*.[cxxx] It means evenness, uprightness, and straightness. Recall that in the Hebrew mindset, *tsadaq* or righteousness means "to walk a straight line." Psalms 143:10 says: "Teach me to do Your will, For You are my God; Let Your good Spirit lead me on level ground."

<u>Equity is something we choose.</u>

"Make straight paths for your feet that the limb which is lame may not be put out of joint but rather be healed" (Hebrews 12:13).

<u>But equity is also something provided by God. It is something He does in us.</u>

"In all your ways acknowledge Him and He will make your path straight" (Proverbs 3:6).

<u>Equity is a moral decision.</u>

"You who are full of all deceit and fraud…will you not cease to make crooked the straight ways of the Lord?" (Acts 13:10).

As we compare "equality" with "equity" we discover that Alinsky and the Bible strongly disagree about what's wrong in America.

For Alinsky, "evil" is institutional, not personal. But surveys reveal that most of our institutions (educational, social, entertainment, media, and political) are sympathetic to his position. Consequently one would think we would already be experiencing his utopia. Of course, Alinsky has a ready response...we can never experience this utopia until everyone has economic equality.

Today this is prevented because, according to Alinsky, "some damn businessman" invented private property, which is the root of every evil.

The thing is, Alinsky's theories have been tested. Historically, Stalin's successful implementation of Alinsky's ideas resulted in the death of 80 million people.

Alinsky motivates his "masses" by appealing to their greed and stirring up old resentments. Greed and strife...two of the seven abominations that God hates (Proverbs 6:16). Not surprisingly, the Bible rejects Alinsky as a "false prophet" of truth (Jeremiah 6:13; 23:36).

The Bible teaches that the problem is not outside of us, it's inside. Recall Jesus' story of the three servants: one is given five talents of gold, another two, and the third, only one.

Alinsky would have taken offense for the third servant, the one who only received one talent. After all, he didn't get his fair share. But Jesus reserved his harshest judgment for this man. In fact, He said that the talent given to him will be taken and given to the one with ten talents (who doubled his five).

How can this be? We'll never understand if we think evil is institutional. Jesus knew this. In the story, the servant loathed the "wealthy man," and used that to justify his sloth. Jesus calls the man wicked and lazy. The problem was never poorness of person. It was always poorness of soul.

Solomon's "Calling" with Alinsky's Vocation

In Proverbs, *chokmah* refers to "wisdom." More specifically it refers to wisdom for successful living. God wants to give us *chokmah*. Many scholars believe *chokmah* is the central message of Proverbs.

Remember Solomon? *Chokmah*, together with discernment, were the two graces God gave Solomon in his dream. Solomon received both of these gifts specifically for one reason…to help him judge Israel. *Chokmah*, then, was given to Solomon to help him in his calling.[cxxxi]

To some degree "callings" are found in the Bible from day one. In Genesis 2:19-20 God waits to see what Adam will "call" the animals. A few verses later Adam "calls" Eve "woman" because she was taken out of man. Later on, he "calls" her "Eve" because she was the mother of all the living (Genesis 2:23). In Genesis 5:29, the man who builds the ark during the flood is "called" Noah ("rest") because that is what he will bring. Abram's ("exalted father") calling is changed in Genesis 17:5 to Abraham ("father of a multitude") to signify his new status. And finally, in Genesis 35:9-10 Jacob, ("supplanter") the one who steals both Esau's birthright and blessing, (Genesis 25:26-31), is given a new "calling" as Israel ("God prevails").

But "callings" don't mean very much in our contemporary culture. That's probably because we tend to think of "vocation" reductively as just the kind of work that we do. But "vocation" is from a 15th century Latin root *vocat-* , past participle of *vocare* "call, name."[cxxxii] For the Christian, "vocation" is your "calling from God," something we discover as we *shema* (listen to and obey) God's heart. And it directly determines what your occupation should be. God offers *chokmah* or "wisdom for successful living" to equip us in that vocation.[cxxxiii]

Alinsky also addressed "calling" but in a very different way. For Alinsky, God's council, wisdom, and direction are all replaced by the state. Alinsky's state guarantees (mandates) and guides (dictates) our vocation producing useful employment (work contrived to ensure that the state survives).

Central to Alinsky's socialist dogma is the guarantee of a "vocation" by the state. But in God's economy, vocations are not party gifts from the state; they are callings from God.

Note that these are all economic valuations. From Chapter Two, we learned that God has quite a bit to say about *economos*.

Let's compare *chokmah* (wisdom for successful living) and Alinsky's vocation:

Chokmah	Alinsky
…favors good sense	…favors the state
…is practical for the individual	…the individual practices what the State requires
…"haves" carefully use goods wisely	…All-wise state plunders goods from "haves" for "have-nots"
…interested in personal outcomes	…personal interests redirected to favor state-designed outcomes

The distinction between the biblical *chokmah* and Alinsky's socialist "vocation" is even more sharply defined when we look at the authority/power structure behind these competitive "truth claims."

For Alinsky, authority is found by whipping the masses into a frenzy, powered by jealousy and selfish ambition. This enables him to seize power and plunder the economic engine, committing theft on a national scale. In Alinsky's mind, taking someone's private goods unlawfully is completely lawful if organized by the State. That apparent contradiction makes sense to Alinsky because morality becomes whatever moves his agenda forward.

Alinsky's agenda is driven by jealousy and selfish ambition. God has already weighed in on Alinsky's schemes.

> But if you have bitter jealousy and selfish ambition in your heart, do not be arrogant and so lie against the truth. This wisdom is not that which comes down from above, but is earthly, natural, demonic. For where jealousy and selfish ambition exist, there is disorder and every evil thing. But the wisdom from above is first pure, then peaceable, gentle, reasonable, full of mercy and good fruits, unwavering, without hypocrisy. And the seed whose fruit is righteousness is sown in peace by those who make peace. (James 3:14-18)

Summary

Together we looked at Saul Alinsky's agenda. We considered four of his nine objectives: righteousness vs. Alinsky's peace; the Bible's justice vs. social justice; equity vs. democratic equality; and *chokmah*/calling vs. Alinsky's sense of vocation. These have been compared with Biblical ideas and found unapologetically hostile to God's truth.

Other comparisons could include "prudence and circumspection" (*sakal*) with "cooperation"; "purpose" (*mezimmah*) with "values that give meaning to life"; "learning and persuasiveness" (*leqach*) with "education"; "direction, counsel, and wise counsel" (*tachbulah*) with "organization which will change the world"; and "fear of the Lord" with "power." These last five are left to the student as an exercise.

I think we can agree that both Alinsky and Solomon introduce over-arching narratives. Both intend to challenge us. Each narrative is revolutionary and mutually exclusive to the other. This is a critical moment in history. Whatever our choice is, we can see that it has the potential to dramatically change us, our children, and our country.

I especially grieve for my black friends in south LA where we lived prior to heading to Africa. These, the disenfranchised, have strongly hailed Alinsky's message. But they also love the Lord, often more deeply than many of my white friends. It will be a test for those whose ancestors were once enslaved to realize that Alinsky is not leading them into freedom, but a new kind of slavery. This new slavery has chains of gold but is in rebellion to God's word: "Righteousness exalts a nation, but sin is a disgrace to any people" (Proverbs 14:34).

EIGHT

Fools and their Folly

"Fools despise wisdom and instruction."

Proverbs 1:7b

It was just a small bump…less than a pea. But now, two months later, it was six times larger and our baby was having a biopsy. As a young surgeon, I watched as they scraped it off my little girl's skull. It was bad.

Histiocytosis X.

The Mayo doctor confirmed my fears. "We'll give her electron beam." I listened as he explained to Colleen what this was. We smash atoms, then bombard the tumor with electrons.

I think when something like this happens, you go into a kind of fog. Even today, I can't recall most of the conversation. My thinking was compartmentalized, fragmented. One side of my brain asked, "What was God doing?" We were on the cusp of returning to Africa. The other side was horrified. I flashed back to a lecture in class. Her skin would fall off, her organs rot out, and then she'd die. Probably six weeks.

We prayed for our little girl to live. When she went bald after the treatment, I irrationally prayed that where the thing had been, the hair would grow in twice as thick. I was mentally clouded. I thought about my medical colleagues. No secret to their disdain toward articles of faith. In post-grad I'd often seen academic prejudice directed at Christians. It mirrored the derision in our culture, a loathing which seethed just beneath a civilized veneer. We were the worst kind of fools, self-deluded into believing worn-out fairytales, and as such not to be trusted.

Was the chance of a recovery for my little girl just another delusion?

****

The wisdom of the world…used by our enemy to steal and kill and destroy. Ironically, the Bible has something to say about that: "For the wisdom of this world is foolishness before God." (1 Corinthians 2:14).

What does that mean—"the wisdom of this world is foolishness before God"?

Well, certainly there are many answers to this. The Bible teaches us over a dozen times that foolishness is practiced by fools.[cxxxiv] So to answer this question let's examine each of these fools more closely.

pethiy	Naïve, "open-minded"[cxxxv]
latson	Scoffers
kesil	Insolence, arrogant
'evil	Evil
naval	Fool, idiot, stupid, dense

In Proverbs we read about five very different kinds of fools. But if we look only at the definitions of the English or even the Hebrew words we would miss out on much of what Solomon wants to tell us. So instead, let us see how these words are used throughout the rest of the Old Testament. When we do that, a very different picture unfolds, a picture remarkable for revealing Satan's strategy to destroy the church. Unfortunately, the large number of passages also results in an unwieldy, overwhelming amount of detail.

While considering this I was surprised one Sunday to recognize portraits of all five fools represented in the story of Christ's crucifixion. The reaction of these groups: bystanders, criminals, soldiers, leaders, and priests, was also remarkable because all five called for Jesus to come off the cross but each for very different reasons. Moreover, their reactions to Christ's death provides a visual mnemonic that can be used to summarize the truth about Proverb's five fools and how Satan uses them to cripple the church.

The Narrative

"When they came to the place called The Skull, there they crucified Him and the criminals, one on the right and the other on the left. But Jesus was saying, 'Father, forgive them; for they do not know what they are doing.' And they cast lots, dividing up His garments among themselves.

And the people stood by, looking on.

And even the rulers were sneering at Him, saying, 'He saved others; let Him save Himself if this is the Christ of God, His Chosen One.'

The soldiers also mocked Him, coming up to Him, offering Him sour wine, and saying, 'If You are the King of the Jews, save Yourself!' Now there was also an inscription above Him, 'This is the King of the Jews.'

One of the criminals who were hanged there was hurling abuse at Him, saying, 'Are You not the Christ? Save Yourself and us!' But the other answered, and rebuking him said, 'Do you not even fear God, since you are under the same sentence of condemnation? And we indeed are suffering justly, for we are receiving what we deserve for our deeds; but this man has done nothing wrong.' And he was saying, 'Jesus, remember me when You come in Your kingdom!'" (Luke 23:26-42; Mark 15:29-32).

Five fools. Each calling for Jesus to get down off the cross…but once again, each for their own very private reasons.

The Pethiy [cxxxvi]

We've discussed this one already. The *pethiy* are simple, naïve, open-minded. They don't get it.

> "[Jesus, describing the crowds] …for they do not know what they are doing…And the people stood by, looking on" (Luke 23:34-35).

> [The crowds taunting Jesus] 'Ha! You who are going to destroy the temple and rebuild it in three days, save Yourself, and come down from the cross!'" (Mark 15:29).

The people once asked Jesus for a "sign" to prove His authority. He replied that if they destroyed "this" temple, He would "raise" it up in three days. The Jews didn't realize Jesus was talking about the temple of His own body. For the Jews, Herod's temple represented God's favor and presence in their lives. They taunted him later at his crucifixion. Having screamed at Pilate to crucify Jesus, they added to their treachery by sneering at His inability to get off the cross, let alone rebuild "the temple."

Isn't it amazing? God's own Son was right in front of them. From childhood, they heard stories of the coming Messiah who would save them. But their spirituality was so wrapped up in the temple stones that they couldn't see (Ezekiel 24:25): "…His glory, glory as of the only begotten from the Father, full of grace and truth" (John 1:14).

People are like that today. Easy spirituality wrapped in the ritual of some pre-packaged religion which then replaces the Bible and a relationship with God. Left with just a form of godliness and focused on rituals, they worship an empty shell.

God asks: How long will you go on being "simple and open-minded" (Proverbs 1:22)?

The Eviyl

The *eviyl* despise wisdom.[cxxxvii] They mock when they are guilty. They are quarrelsome, licentious: "**One** of the **criminals** who were **hanged** there was **hurling abuse** at Him…**Save Yourself** and us!" (Luke 23:39; bold emphasis mine).

Hanging next to this thief was the One who could have saved his soul, but his only thought is to save his own skin. He was blinded by rage in a prison made of his own hate. He focuses this rage against God: "The [*eviyl*] foolishness of man ruins his way, and his heart rages against the LORD" (Proverbs 19:3).

Today the *eviyl* are still wrapped up and captured by their sin, mocking, quarrelsome, and promiscuous.

The Latsown[cxxxviii]

"And [the soldiers] cast lots, dividing His garments among them. 'Hail, King of the Jews!'" (Mark 15:18)

The *latsown* have an exaggerated sense of their importance/abilities. The soldiers' training was to carry out orders, and yet this was sport for them. Thus they mocked Jesus by hailing Him as a king, an order giver: "The soldiers also mocked Him, coming up to Him, offering Him sour wine, and saying, 'If You are the King of the Jews, save Yourself'" (Luke 23:36).

The soldiers weren't interested in Jesus' kingship. If they had to crucify Jesus, they were going to have some sport. They'd show this nomadic preacher what real authority was.

We find additional insight in Proverbs: "…scoffers delight themselves in their scoffing" (Proverbs 1:22).

This verse references "scoffers." In Chapter Three, I promised to return to this passage because of its translation problems. Does "Lilith" ring a bell? The first time scoffers are referenced in this verse, it comes from *Liyliyth,* not *latsown,* as it does at the end of the verse. *Liyliyth* is defined by Strong's as a female goddess known as a night demon who haunts the desolate places of Edom.[cxxxix] At the very minimum that has to startle you. But it's not surprising when you consider that scoffers place themselves above what they scoff at, in this case, God. 1 Samuel 15:23 says rebellion (against God) is as the sin of witchcraft. Why would it not be? As pointed out by Alinsky in the last chapter, Satan was the first rebel. So it's not unexpected that one who scoffs at God would be vulnerable to satanic control.

Today the arrogant still mock God's word. They aren't interested in pretend spiritual authority. They serve power and they're ready to ensure everyone knows it. Ironically they are blind to the power of Satan over their lives.

The Keciyl[cxl]

We've learned with the "open-minded" (*pethiy*) that God has a different perspective than we do. We see this again with the *keciyl*, fools who "hate the knowledge of God" (Proverbs 1:7). The *keciyl* are also marked by these characteristics:

> …Not interested in wisdom, just their view of the world, base right/wrong on their feelings, angry when things don't go their way, exploit others to get work done, empty spirituality, use words to promote their reality, pursue unjust wealth, live in ease and prosperity, have money but no wisdom.[cxli]

In the story of the crucifixion, the rulers, or *archons*, are examples of the *keciyl*: "…the rulers [the *archon*] were sneering at Him…if this is the Christ of God, His Chosen One [*eklektos*]" (Luke 23:35)

Solomon's example of *archon* who were *keciyl*

> "A poor yet wise lad is better than an old and foolish (*keciyl*) king who no longer knows how to receive instruction" (Ecclesiastes 4:13, compare 2 Chronicles 25:16, Psalm 107:11, Proverbs 19:21, 21:30).

> "…you acted in ignorance (*agnoia*, moral blindness), just as your rulers (*archon*) did also" (Acts 3:17).

"...the wisdom which none of the rulers of this age has understood; for if they had understood it they would not have crucified the Lord of glory..." (1 Corinthians 2:8).

These were the *archon*, the rulers. As such, they were obsessed with hierarchy. They despise God's knowledge. They only desired power. So when they mocked Jesus, they asked, are you *eklektos*,[cxlii] (the most exalted office conceivable)? Are you powerful? If so, then we, the powerful, will receive you, honor you...if you have the power.

People today make "power" their god. They mock people of faith. God considers them *keciyl*, dullards and simpletons. They don't simply reject God. They hate even the knowledge of Him. Proverbs says their wealth and comfort will destroy them.[cxliii]

The Naval[cxliv]

"Thus says the Lord GOD, 'Woe to the foolish [*naval*] prophets who are following their own spirit and have seen nothing" (Ezekiel 13:3).

"The chief priests also, along with the scribes, were mocking among themselves...'He saved others; He cannot save Himself.' 'Let this Christ, the King of Israel, now come down from the cross, so that we may see and believe!'" (Mark 15:31-32).

Notice the irony, "...so that we may... believe." These priests weren't interested in belief. They had just condemned Jesus to death at the very time when Jesus claimed to be God's Son.

Deuteronomy 32:15 says: "[The *naval*] scorned the Rock of his salvation." Isaiah 32:6 adds: "[The *naval*] speaks nonsense, and his heart inclines toward wickedness: to practice ungodliness and to speak error against the LORD, to keep the hungry person unsatisfied and to withhold drink from the thirsty leaving the parishioners thirsty and hungry."

How can this be? Why would the priests scorn Jesus, the Rock of their salvation, leaving "the parishioners thirsty and hungry"? Pilate understood: "They delivered Him up because of envy" (Matthew 27:18).

Who are the *naval* today? They're often the ones we honor: religious, academic, and cultural icons (Isaiah 32:5-6). They might seem amazing, but they reject God's word, and God rejects them.

The five fools: the open-minded fools, the evil fools, the scorners, the arrogant fools, and the insolent, morally corrupt fools.

****

We clung to our tiny daughter, helplessly watching her slip away. My wife looked at the pink lacy dress our baby would never wear. She began to cry. We learned to take one day at a time. To spend that one day rejoicing in our baby's life.

Then, as we watched, the hair right next to the scar began to grow. It grew in twice as thick…just like my prayer. Set in the middle of her bald head it looked like a button-hole.[cxlv] The power of God. The Mayo Clinic followed her for about a year. Then they discharged her, said our own doctor could do that.

Today, 31 years later, Alyssa is still precious to us.

Christ crucified…to them it is foolishness, but to us, the power of God.

> "But we preach Christ crucified, to Jews a stumbling block and to Gentiles foolishness, but to those who are the called, both Jews and Greeks, Christ the power of God and the wisdom of God" (1 Corinthians 1:23).

NINE

Mirror, Mirror, On the Wall

"I, wisdom, dwell with prudence."

Proverbs 8:12

I tried not to stare. Three fresh gallbladders hung loosely from his head. *Imfene*...a witch doctor. I shuddered as I listened to his broken English. I thought of the young mothers I had seen after their botched care. They arrived in shock, their wombs ruptured; dead babies floating in their bellies. I thought of the young boy that wandered around the hospital. His mind was gone. He could not speak. The imfene had told the father he must eat his son's tongue if he wanted his business to prosper. And worse...much, much worse...the work of Satan, our enemy.

****

The previous seven chapters have taken us on a journey through his mind. He uses the worldview of the *keciyl*, the seductive hatred of the *eviyl*, ridicule from the *latsown*, and the insolent moral corruption of the *naval*. Why?

The enemy wants to enslave you. He comes to steal, kill, and destroy.

And he uses the "open-mindedness" of the *pethiy*.

Our culture venerates the open-minded. We call them free-thinkers, liberal, tolerant, unbigoted, advanced. The list goes on. Webster's says the "open-minded" are "receptive to arguments or ideas."

Being "open-minded" sounds pretty cool, right? Who doesn't want to be perceived as being reasonable? Moreover, the alternative, "narrow-mindedness," appears to be the only other option. Who hasn't heard this stinging rebuke directed at themselves or fellow Christians? "Judge not lest you be judgmental"[cxlvi] (modern rendition of Matthew 7:1).

You'll be told you can't help your narrow-mindedness: "For the gate is small and the way is narrow that leads to life, and there are few who find it" (Matthew 7:14).

Do you want life? The way is narrow so you must "narrow" your thinking to find it.[cxlvii] It's in your DNA as a Christian.

Linking "religious beliefs" to narrow-mindedness is an automatic reflex as seen at the Urban Dictionary which includes this colorful ad hominem:

> Narrow-mindedness: a person or persons who cannot see beyond their own set of values and/or will not accept them. Is often related to religious matters, where people cannot accept the other religion's beliefs. It often happens where one is in ignorance.

Overlooking the creative grammar, how should we respond? Naively, many Christians nuance "narrow-mindedness" and "truth." They usually finish with the classic "tu quoque,"[cxlviii] accusing their accusers of being "narrow-minded."

Like a mental game of hot potato, nobody wants to be perceived as the one whose mind is "narrow."

Proverbs 26:4 reveals a more excellent way: "Do not answer a fool according to his folly, or you will also be like him."

This verse is telling us not to get sucked in. When we do it begins to resemble the kindergarten kid who is called a nincompoop. His response? "I know you are, but what am I?"

Alright, then what are we supposed to do? The solution is in the next verse: "Answer a fool as his folly deserves, that he not be wise in his own eyes" (Proverbs 26:5).

Proverbs 26:5 directs us to think strategically. The simple truth is that their argument is not just silly, it's wrong.

God never calls us to "narrow-mindedness." Again? We're not called to "narrow-mindedness." Being told that "open-mindedness" is against God's plan is not the same as being called to "narrow-mindedness." God's word leads us in an entirely different direction.

Hopefully if you've read the book this far, you're at least curious about what that means. For the answer we're going to Chapter One of Proverbs: "...To give prudence ('ormah) to the "open-minded" (Proverbs 1:4).

Prudence! Yes, and God offers it ('ormah Proverbs 1:4) to the open-minded, and together with circumspection (sakal Proverbs 1:3) to those with discipline.[cxlix] Either way, I'm guessing "prudence" is not on your bucket list. And while "prudence" can get us where we need to go, "shrewdness," Strong's first choice in the definition is easier to understand.[cl]

Aristotle understood this. Moreover, he said "shrewdness" (phronesis) was essential if we wanted to achieve the highest wisdom.[cli]

Prophesy adds that Jesus' character is defined by shrewdness (sakal Jeremiah 23:5).

Not once, but twice we are told that God is searching everywhere to find those who have shrewdness (sakal Psalm 14:2, 53:2).

And that's why it's not surprising when, during his ministry, Jesus grieved that Christians were lacking shrewdness (phronesis Luke 16:8).[clii]

And finally Daniel explains that in the end-times those who have shrewdness will be leaders and will "shine brightly like the brightness of the expanse of heaven" (*sakal* Daniel 12:3).

But none of that makes any difference if you're not really sure what "shrewdness" means. So let's ask Webster's Dictionary.[cliii] Shrewdness: marked by "clever discerning awareness."[cliv]

Okay, so now we know:

Webster's says that "shrewdness" is marked by clever awareness.

Aristotle, the great philosopher, said the highest wisdom could not be achieved without clever awareness.

Proverbs, the Book of Wisdom says that clever awareness is indispensable for those who have become "open-minded."

Jesus, the Son of God had clever awareness and grieved because Christians didn't.

And finally, we learn that God is looking for those with clever awareness; they will be His leaders.

Are you beginning to connect the dots? No? Okay…think of your own kids.

How many of you would ever teach them "open-mindedness" when it comes to strangers with candy? No? Well, it's the same with God: "Do not be carried away by varied and strange teachings; for it is good for the heart to be strengthened by grace, not by foods, through which those who were so occupied were not benefited" (Hebrews 13:9).

God warns you not to cozy up to strange teachings. Don't be narrow-minded either: be **"cleverly aware"**: "But examine everything carefully; hold fast to that which is good" (1 Thessalonians 5:21).

In fact, God promises in Proverbs 1:4 and 14:15 that this clever awareness can both protect us from strange teachings and also restore us if we've been "open-minded." Proverbs 1:4 says: "To give ['*ormah*, clever awareness] to the [*pethiy*, open-minded] naïve." Proverbs 14:15

adds: "The [*pethiy*, open-minded] naïve believe everything, but a ['*aruwm*, related to '*ormah*, cleverly discerning aware] man [considers his steps]."

Still not impressed? You should be. Why? What's so important? What's at stake?

In the first chapter, I challenged God to prove that He was real. I had my doubts about whether it could hold up to scrutiny.

Well, I wasn't alone with these doubts. In three different studies, surveyors asked teens if they believed the Bible. I averaged the studies to get a single number. What did you think it was? <u>Twenty-five percent!</u>[clv] "Only one in four teens still believe the Bible![clvi]

Our youth reject the Bible as a source of knowledge. God grieves this: "My people are destroyed for lack of knowledge. Because you have rejected knowledge, I also will reject you from being My priest. Since you have forgotten the law of your God, I also will forget your children" (Hosea 4:6).

How did this happen? To find out why our kids are turning their backs on God and the church, we need to take a closer look at the five fools of Proverbs.

The Pethiy

We already know from Chapter One that "open-mindedness" (*pethiy*) leads directly to "apostasy," i.e. Christians leaving God. Moreover, from the discussion above, you know both the "prevention" and the "cure" is clever awareness.

But open-mindedness isn't the only reason our kids abandon God. Those other reasons are found when we look at the remaining fools of Proverbs.

The 'Eviyl

The *'eviyl*, translated "fool," despise authority. They will go out of their way to steal your peace. Right or wrong, they'll argue any point, laughing or raging until they get your goat. They're completely immoral. They mock your values. They won't listen; they're certainly not going to follow God's instructions.[clvii]

Be careful. They'll try to knock you off your game, challenge you to loosen up, embrace any bit of sin.

Remember the story of Balaam in Numbers. King Balak, faced with a million invading Jews, hired Balaam, the prophet, to curse Israel. God instead had Balaam blessing Israel.

Balaam had a problem. He wasn't getting any gold from Balak by doing it God's way. Even more, he knew he couldn't curse Israel while they were under God's protection. So Balaam hatched a plan. He got Israel to compromise, to sin a bit (Numbers 31:16). When they did, God's protection evaporated and Israel paid a terrible price.

The *'eviyl* are:

> ...like unreasoning animals...They are stains and blemishes, reveling in their deceptions, as they carouse with you, having eyes full of adultery that never cease from sin, enticing unstable souls, having a heart trained in greed, accursed children; forsaking the right way, they have gone astray, having followed the way of Balaam, the son of Beor, who loved the wages of unrighteousness...For speaking out arrogant words of vanity they entice by fleshly desires, by sensuality, those who barely escape from the ones who live in error, promising them freedom while they themselves are slaves of corruption; for by what a man is overcome, by this he is enslaved. (2 Peter 2:12-19)

The *'eviyl*, like Balaam, get Christians to compromise with sin, leading them back to slavery:

> For if, after they have escaped the defilements of the world by the knowledge of the Lord and Savior Jesus Christ, they are again entangled in them and are overcome, the last state has become worse for them than the first. For it would be better for them not to have known the way of righteousness, than having known it,

to turn away from the holy commandment handed on to them. It has happened to them according to the true proverb, "A dog returns to its own vomit," and, "A sow, after washing, returns to wallowing in the mire." (2 Peter 2:20-22)

Then how are we going to find victory? Remember how Balaam defeated Israel by getting them to sin "a bit." The rest of the passage tells us how to remain under God's protection: "…then the Lord knows how to rescue the godly from temptation, and to keep the unrighteous under punishment for the day of judgment, and especially those who indulge the flesh in its corrupt desires and despise authority" (2 Peter 2:9-10).

The Latsown

Scoffers (*latsown*) rebel against the knowledge of God. We discovered previously that they're satanically influenced. The *latsown*'s weapon is ridicule, described by Saul Alinsky as the rebel's more powerful tool. As Proverbs 29:8 explains, "Scorners set a city aflame…" Do not underestimate them.[clviii]

On our own, we are vulnerable. But God's word promises protection. Proverbs 3:34 says, "Though He scoffs at the scoffers, Yet He gives grace to the afflicted." 2 Thessalonians 1:6 adds: "For after all it is only just for God to repay with affliction those who afflict you."

Consider Nehemiah, cupbearer to King Artaxerxes. He was charged by God to rebuild the wall around Jerusalem. But Sanballat and Tobiah were determined to thwart him. Nehemiah responded to their open threats and ridicule by reviewing his purpose and relationship to God.

His first response to them was: "The God of heaven will give us success; therefore we His servants will arise and build, but you have no portion, right or memorial in Jerusalem" (Nehemiah 2:20).

When they tried to lure Nehemiah away from the wall and into a trap, he said: "I am doing a great work and I cannot come down. Why should the work stop while I leave it and come down to you?" (Nehemiah 6:3).

In response to accusations that the Jews were planning to rebel, Nehemiah said: "For all of them were trying to frighten us, thinking, 'They will become discouraged with the work and it will not be done.' But now, O God, strengthen my hands" (Nehemiah 6:20).

Nehemiah overturned the people's discouragement. He strategized against the plans of the enemy. He challenged people to renew their spirituality by abolishing usury. He confronted the governors; pressing them to lessen the taxes. He rebuffed attempts by Sanballat and Tobiah to frighten him.

Nehemiah's actions illustrate Proverbs 2:1-10. I encourage you to spend time reading this. A much too shortened version is that God gives wisdom, knowledge, and understanding which then enable us (and Nehemiah) to practice righteousness, justice, and equity. Now drop down to verse 11: "Understanding will watch over you, to deliver you from the way of evil, **from the man who speaks perverse things**; the scoffer" (Proverbs 2:11; bold emphasis mine).[clix]

Postscript

This last discussion is not an empty exercise. Think about your kids. How can they handle scorn, or as we now call it, peer pressure? The same way Nehemiah did: through relationship and purpose. Let's take a look at those two things in Proverbs 1:1-4.

> The proverbs of Solomon the son of David, king of Israel: To know wisdom and instruction, To discern the sayings of understanding, To receive instruction in wise behavior, Righteousness, justice and equity; To give prudence to the naive, To the youth knowledge (*da'ath*) and discretion (*mezimmah*).

Relational Knowledge

Da'ath in verse four is translated "knowledge." But it is incredibly more than learning more stuff about God. The root from which we get *da'ath* is *yada*, the verb used to describe sexual intimacy. *Da'ath*, then describes an intimate, experiential, relational knowledge of God which change every relationship in their lives. The entire next chapter in Proverbs explains how this brings life and security to the young believer. It's relational, up close. This relational knowledge allows our youth to experience the power and presence of a living Father together with relationships with those around him/her.

Purpose

Strong's translates *mezimmah* as purpose. [clx] Jesus was big on purpose. Recall Jesus' response to a very unsettled Martha: "Martha, Martha, you are worried and bothered about so many things; but only one thing is necessary…" (Luke 10:41-42).

What is that one thing? It's our purpose. <u>And that pulls us back to relationship.</u>

Take a look at the parable of the rich young ruler. The entire story bears repeating.

> And a lawyer stood up and put Him to the test, saying, "Teacher, what shall I do to inherit eternal life?" And He said to him, "What is written in the Law? How does it read to you?" And he answered, **"You shall love the Lord your God with all your heart, and with all your soul, and with all your strength, and with all your mind; And your neighbor as yourself."** And He said to him, **"You have answered correctly; "Do this and you will live."** (Luke 10:25-28; bold emphasis mine)

The lawyer's response echoes Deuteronomy 6:5 (called the *shema* by devout Jews): "Hear, O Israel! The **Lord** is our God, the **Lord** is one! 'You shall love the **Lord** your God with all your heart and with all your soul and with all your might.'"

It also reflects Leviticus 19:18: "…but love your neighbor as yourself." [clxi]

In Matthew 22:40, Jesus explains that the entire Law as well as the Prophetic writings depend on those two verses. You want to know your purpose? Read and *shema* (hear and obey) God's Word, the Bible: "He who has My commandments and keeps them is the one who loves

Me; and he who loves Me will be loved by My Father, and I will love him and will disclose Myself to him" (John 14:21).

Finally, take a look at Proverbs 3:21-24 where we see the exalted value of <u>purpose</u> for our children.

> My son, let them not vanish from your sight; Keep sound wisdom and discretion [**purpose**], So they will be life to your soul And adornment to your neck. Then you will walk in your way securely, And your foot will not stumble. When you lie down, you will not be afraid; When you lie down, your sleep will be sweet. (bold emphasis mine)

Protection from peer pressure…found in relationship and purpose. Do you find it ironic that our kids are searching high and low for relationship and purpose but don't bother looking at Proverbs where it is placed in plain sight, together with security in God?

The Keciyl

From other passages[clxii] we learn that the *keciyl* (i.e. the insolent, arrogant fool) are not interested in wisdom, just their own *view of the world*. They base right and wrong on their feelings and are angry when things don't go their way. They exploit others to get work done. Theirs is empty spirituality, which they promote with words. They pursue unjust wealth, living in ease and prosperity.

The verse which best summarizes the *keciyl* is Proverbs 1:22: "And fools (*keciyl*) hate knowledge." The "knowledge" which they hate is *da'ath*, that "intimate relational knowledge of God" that we discussed earlier. Their <u>worldview</u> begins and ends with hatred of this "knowledge," and then looks elsewhere for truth. The Bible rightly calls them dullards and simpletons.

So why do they hate God's knowledge? Proverbs 1:32 gives us both the reason and the outcome: "And the complacency of fools will destroy them."

Shalvah, translated complacency, also references ease and prosperity. As the *keciyl* embrace the mentality of the world, they are rewarded with carefree prosperity. But Proverbs 1:32 explains that their outcome is certain.

In sharp contrast to their worldview, the "knowledge of God" (*da'ath*) is inexhaustible. But, like the *keciyl's* view, it too is a worldview.

A worldview? Yes. A worldview. The truth is that everyone (including the Christian) has an understanding which enables them to engage reality. This understanding is called a worldview.

So what happens when worldviews clash? To properly understand you need to recognize that worldviews don't just hang in space; they're based upon assumptions.

For the Christian, those assumptions are more accurately called beliefs, and are based upon revealed knowledge found in the Bible. Those attacking Christian beliefs also have their own worldview and that's where the fun begins.

If your opponents are clever, they'll keep their assumptions hidden so they can manipulate the results. We've already seen what this looks like with natural selection, "living dirt," and scientism.

This may seem formidable because quite often their worldviews are long and drawn out. Their assumptions are another matter. For example, the claims of postmodernism all boil down to one assumption: truths which are true for everyone don't exist. That's funny, because they assume that everyone agrees, that is, that this "truth" is true for everyone. But mandating their claim to be universally true means it cannot be true by its own definition...ironically making postmodernism self-referentially absurd.

There are many excellent books exposing the hidden assumptions of these hostile worldviews. You need to educate yourself. This is not as hard as it might seem since most worldviews boil down to just a few general types.

When you do this you're going to need a few ground rules.

First, watch out for your own weaknesses "Brethren, even if anyone is caught in any trespass, you who are spiritual, restore such a one in a spirit of gentleness; each one looking to yourself, so that you too will not be tempted" (Galatians 6:1).

Second, talk out of relationship. Too many people blast away at the very ones who need our compassion. Relate to them: "As a result, we are no longer to be children, tossed here and there by waves and carried about by every wind of doctrine, by the trickery of men, by craftiness in deceitful scheming; but speaking the truth in love..." (Ephesians 4:14-15).

Third, be gentle. As 2 Timothy 2:24 says: "The Lord's bond-servant must not be quarrelsome, but be kind to all, able to teach, patient when wronged, with gentleness correcting those who are in opposition." 1 Peter 3:15 further adds: "...Always being ready to make a defense to everyone who asks you to give an account for the hope that is in you, yet with gentleness and reverence." Finally, Colossians 4:6 says, "Let your speech always be with grace so that you will know how to respond to each person."

Fourth, remember, we're not trying to win an argument: "Remind them of these things, and solemnly charge them in the presence of God not to wrangle about words, which is useless and leads to the ruin of the hearers" (2 Timothy 2:14).

Fifth, we're instead trying to set someone free: "...if perhaps God may grant them repentance leading to the knowledge of the truth, and they may come to their senses and escape from the snare of the devil, having been held captive by him to do his will" (2 Timothy 2:24-25).

Finally I'd like to pass on something borrowed from Dr. Jeff Myers at Bryan College. Dr. Myers taught Christian youth of all ages two simple questions.

1. What do you mean by that?

2. How do you know that's true?

Myers once sent first graders prepared with this training in to watch a paleontologist at a museum of natural history. The kids, armed with their two questions, naively asked what she was doing. This Ph.D. trained scientist then launched into a wonderful explanation of fossils and how they confirmed that evolution was true.

The kids simply asked: How do you know that's true? This was followed by another explanation, equally eloquent.

About five questions deep, the paleontologist, now exasperated finally said: "Because I know."

Assumptions.

The Naval

In their innermost being, the *naval* reason that there is no God: "The fool (*naval*) has said in his heart, 'There is no God'" (Psalm 14:1).

The *naval* don't simply reject God. They reject His very existence. They reject His commands (verse one) and they reject His people (verse four). Why do they need to do that? The answer is found in the rest of Psalms 14, which I explain below.

Their Agenda: Moral Corruption

The *naval* are ethically corrupt (*ta'ab*). They commit abominable deeds (verse one). They have turned aside; they are (*'alach*), morally corrupt (verse three).

So let's use this new information and substitute the word "fool" found in Psalm 14:1 with "moral corrupt person". Now the verse reads, "The [morally corrupt person] has said in his heart, 'There is no God.'"

Now it begins to make sense. These guys have a hidden agenda; they are morally corrupt. They don't want God looking over their shoulder, judging their behavior. As Dostoevsky's character Dimitri in the *Brothers Karamazov* famously mused: If there is no God, everything is permitted.[clxiii]

The point is that God gives us healthy ways to satisfy our appetites (which He also gave us). But if there was no God then men, for example, could sexually molest women without guilt or repercussion. In fact, Darwin's survival of the fittest would demand they do so to ensure their survival in the gene pool. I'm not making this stuff up. Time Magazine, in the not so distant past, suggested such behavior would be acceptable for this very reason.[clxiv]

Proverbs 29:18 agrees with Dostoevsky. Without God, people could do anything (pedophilia, murder, etc.) that they wanted without consequences: "Where there is no vision (divine guidance), the people are unrestrained…" (Proverbs 29:18).

You might think that the *eviyl* and the *naval* are alike. It is true that they are similar; they are both morally corrupt. One large difference is that the *eviyl* seduce you with sin from without whereas the *naval* are seduced by their own heart.

What should we do to protect our children, to protect ourselves? The solution and prevention are the same. Since its straight-forward I'll simply recall the verse.

> How can a young man keep his way pure? By keeping it according to Your word. With all my heart I have sought You; Do not let me wander from Your commandments. Your word I have treasured in my heart, that I may not sin against You. (Psalms 119:9-11)

Summary

In summary, the book of Proverbs is about wisdom. God shouts it out…in our homes, at work, at school, in the government, and in our courts (Proverbs 1:20-21).

You can bet that our enemy will concentrate his efforts in these same areas. Much like in the day of Nehemiah, "…the wall of Jerusalem is broken down and its gates are burned with fire" (Nehemiah 1:3).

Our walls are also broken down; the enemy is already inside the gate.

Nehemiah's response was to pray to God to deliver Israel. God also wants to deliver you. He <u>shouts</u> for you to *shema* His heart.

Can you hear Him?

Or perhaps you've already been "open-minded." Possibly a "Balaam" has brought compromise into your life. Maybe you've been subdued by the comfort of thinking like the world, or intimidated by the power politics of scoffers, or even seduced by your appetites which are inflamed by insolence and moral corruption.

Many years ago, I sat in a jail cell praying to a God I wasn't sure was there. I challenged Him to be real. I said that if He was, then the Bible was going to prove it.

Shortly, I discovered what I already knew. Life was bad.

But I began to see that God is more powerful than the bad. And I discovered that we don't really challenge God's word; God's word challenges us...at the same time bringing clarity to this twisted world.

Many years later, I was speaking to student nurses at our African mission hospital about that very same Word.

I waited until I had everybody's attention and then abruptly said: "You know...I don't really care if the blacks in your country go to hell or not."

It got very quiet.

Why would I say this? The answer is that God's word is a mirror; and it was reflecting my life back at me. Looking into that mirror, I saw months and even years of talking the talk and very little else.

I then told these students that when I realized this was true about me, I got down on my knees and confessed it as sin. I then confessed a second sin to God. I told God that I would never care unless He put His heart for them in me. Guess what? That's what He did. And afterward, I did as well.

God's word is a mirror (James 1:22-25). Those desiring to know God's heart understand this.

> But prove yourselves doers of the word, and not merely
> hearers who delude themselves. For if anyone is a
> hearer of the word and not a doer, he is like a man who

looks at his natural face in a mirror; but once he has looked at himself and gone away, he has immediately forgotten what kind of person he was. But one who looks intently at the perfect law, the law of liberty, and abides by it, not having become a forgetful hearer but an effectual doer, this man will be blessed in what he does. (James 1:22-25).

You want to really know if you've been "open-minded?" Look at yourself in God's mirror. See if you believe what God says you should. And if not, maybe you need to get down on your knees. Let's be among those for whom God is looking, when He looks down from heaven upon the sons of man (Psalms 53:2; also 14:2)...for the cleverly aware (*sakal*) who seek after God.

Appendix A: The Problem of Disorder

Day One through Three

Genesis has two separate creation stories, both written by Moses. But there are three more outside of Genesis which are all written by other biblical authors. Taken together, the five stories are complementary and fill in many details about creation. The account in Job 38 concentrates on the order of land, sea, and atmosphere. Psalm 104 takes us from the small hills of earth to the primordial ocean and then to the formation of continents. Finally, Proverbs 8 gives us day one through three, both in reverse then in chronological order.

The language in Genesis is often confusing. Fortunately, we have some cheats…three completely independent sources which explain what happened and when in those critical first few days.

> Or who enclosed the sea with doors When, bursting forth, it went out from the womb; When I made a cloud its garment And thick darkness its swaddling band, And I placed boundaries on it And set a bolt and doors, And I said, "Thus far you shall come, but no farther; And here shall your proud waves stop?" (Job 38:8-11)

> He established the earth upon its foundations, So that it will not totter forever and ever.
> You covered it with the deep as with a garment;
> The waters were standing above the mountains/hills.
> At Your rebuke they fled, At the sound of
> Your thunder they hurried away.
> The mountains rose; the valleys sank down To
> the place which You established for them.
> You set a boundary that they may not pass over, So that they will not return to cover the earth. (Psalms 104:5-9)

> While He had not yet made the earth and the fields, Nor the first dust of the world. When He established the

heavens, I (wisdom) was there, when He inscribed a circle on the face of the deep, when He made firm the skies above, when the springs of the deep became fixed, when He set for the sea its boundary so that the water would not transgress His command. (Proverbs 8:26-29)

Both Genesis and Proverbs begin by telling us that this is how God establishes/prepares the heavens.

"In the beginning God created the heavens and the earth" [merism referring to the universe] (Genesis 1:1).

The heavens are established[cliv] (*kuwn* "prepared," i.e. 1 Chronicles 22:5 preparations to build temple, 2 Chronicles 26:14 prepared for war [Proverbs 8:27, chronological order]).

- First event, there was no earth.
  - The earth was *tohu wa bohu*, ("nothingness" and "empty space") (Genesis 1:2).
  - "While He had not yet made the earth and the fields, Nor the first dust of the world" (Proverbs 8:26, chronological order).
  - Jewish scholars two centuries before Christ translating their native Hebrew into Greek rendered *tohu* and *bohu* as *aoratos*, "invisible" and *akataskeuastos*, "unprepared." [clxv]
  - "By faith we understand that the worlds were prepared by the word of God, so that what is seen was not made out of things which are visible" (Hebrews 11:3).
    - Often incorrectly taught that this says the universe was made from nothing (*ex nihilo*).
    - Cannot mean *ex nihilo* because the pattern (repeated over 100 times) in Hebrew 11 is putting something real but not visible into something else.
    - Applying this pattern to Hebrews 11:3 the seen universe is made of an unseen real something. It is not made from nothingness.
- Second event, the surface of the deep.

- - Darkness was over the surface of the deep (Genesis 1:2).
    - "The deep" in this context represents the primordial particles.
      - Particles in "deep" existed as primeval ocean *tehown* (Genesis 1:2).
      - "…what is seen was not made out of things which are visible" (Hebrews 11:3b).
    - The Spirit moves over the face of the deep.
      - Squeezing them into a singularity.
      - "…on the face of the deep" (Proverbs 8:27, chronological order).
- Third event, "let there be light."
  - God's voice unleashes the explosive power of the Big Bang (Genesis 1:3).
  - God characterizes the explosion/light as good *towb*, having design built into it (waters above and below).
- Fourth event: creation of time.
  - God called the light "day" (*yowm*) (Genesis 1:5).
  - *Yowm* also means "time."
- Fifth event: Explosive power of Big Bang creates the expanse.
  - "Let there be an expanse…" (Genesis 1:6).
  - "…in the midst of the waters" consists of primordial particles.
- Sixth event: non-visible waters *above* create the universe in eons of time.
  - "…separated the waters which were below the expanse from the waters which were above the expanse…" (Genesis 1:7).
  - *Min* amplifying waters means: out of which something is made.
  - Prepared in "eons" of time by the word of God (Hebrews 11:3a).
  - Non-visible particles: "…so that what is seen was not made out of things which are visible" (Hebrews 11:3b).
- Seventh event: non-visible waters *below* produce "earth."
  - Circle inscribed on the surface of the deep.

- "It is He who sits above the circle of the earth..." (Isaiah 40:22).
  - Confirms earth is created after the deep (Proverbs 8:27, chronological order).
- Eighth event: creation of land.
  - "...it went out from the womb (i.e. land)" (Job 38:9).
  - Made firm the dust, out of which something is made *shachaq min* (Proverbs 8:28, chronological order).
  - *Shachaq* (Strong's) is best translated as "dust."
  - Translating *shachaq* as "sky" creates nonsense.
  - When there were no mountains, fields, or dust (Proverbs 8:25-26, reverse order).
- Ninth event: springs of the deep.
  - Refers to "springs" (Job 38:8) which would "burst forth" creating "seas."
  - "Or who enclosed the sea with doors..." (Job 38:9).
  - "Have you entered into the springs of the sea or walked in the recesses of the deep?" (Job 38:16).
  - "When there were no springs abounding with water" (Proverbs 8:24b, reverse order).
  - "Springs of the deep become fixed (*'azaz* strong), (Proverbs 8:28, chronological order).
- Tenth event: creation of a primordial sea which covered the earth.
  - "You covered it with the deep as with a garment; the waters were standing above the mountains/hills" (Psalm 104:6).
  - These waters, called the deep, covered the entire earth. (Psalm 104:9)
  - Robert C. Newman, Ph.D., notes that if the earth was flat it would be covered with two miles of water.
- Eleventh event: creation of the sky.
  - Created on day three, together with land and water (Genesis 1:10, Job 38:8-10).
  - "When I made a cloud its garment" (Job 38:9).
  - "And thick darkness its swaddling band" (Job 38:9).

[142]

- Twelfth event: possibly the creation of the continents and separate oceans as the mountains were increased and the sea beds dropped
  - "The mountains rose; the valleys sank down to the place which You established for them" (Psalm 104:8).
  - Creation of individual oceans: "gathered into one place" (Genesis 1:9)
  - Creation of land continents: "let the dry land appear" (Genesis 1:9).
  - Creation of continents and individual oceans: "for the sea its boundary" (Proverbs 8:29).
  - "You set a boundary that they may not pass over, so that they [oceans] will not return to cover the earth" (Psalm 104:9)
  - "For the sea its boundary" (Proverbs 8:29).
  - "And I placed boundaries on it" (Job 38:10).
  - "Here shall your proud waves stop" (Job 38:11)
  - "When He marked out the foundations of the earth" (Proverbs 8:29, compare Psalm 18:15).

As humans we want to make sense of things. The result is that we often impose our will on the text and miss what God has to say. Having all five creation accounts releases scripture to mold our understanding of what God did rather than the other way around. See Appendix C: The Chicken and the Egg and Appendix G: Timing is Everything).

APPENDIX B: The Expanse Expanded

Day Two through Day Four

In Genesis 1:8 God calls the expanse separating the waters "heaven." But ambiguity exists because the Bible uses the same Hebrew word to describe three different heavens. The first heaven represents only the earth's atmosphere. The second heaven contains the entire universe excluding the earth and its atmosphere. The final heaven would be God's throne room (the third heaven described by Paul).

I had always thought the expanse from verse 8 referred to the universe. My impression was reinforced by its use three more times in this same passage (Genesis 1:14-15, 17). Much later I discovered that Seven Day and many Old Earth Creationists instead use the single verse (Genesis 1:20) which identifies the expanse as earth's atmosphere. Their opinion, if correct, would mean that the earth's creation would continue two more days before God calls the dry land "earth."

That, of course, changes the initial conditions specified by the SDC where things are done instantaneously and appointed by individual days. It also violates the language in Proverbs 8:24-29 when God describes creation in both in reverse and chronological order. And it ignores the language in Hebrews 11:3 where we learn that the earth was made from a real something (waters 2 Peter 3:5), but a something which could not be seen. Finally, it means the earth was made before the sun with the issue of killing any vegetation with temperatures hundreds of degrees below zero (see discussion of light in text).

When we find ambiguity like this, it's natural to impose our will on the text. We want to know about beginnings; it is God, Himself who set eternity in our hearts (Ecclesiastes 3:11). But that just highlights the importance of not simply looking at context but also companion verses to discern God's mind. Doing this here resolves the expanse/heaven as the universe.

Appendix C: The Chicken and the Egg

Day Three

- And that brings us to the age old question…which came first, the chicken or the egg…or, in this case, the land or the seas?
- The answer seems pretty straightforward and it's the one accepted by our mainstream churches today.
  - In Genesis 1:9 we read: "let the waters below the heaven be gathered into one place and let the dry land appear."
  - 2 Peter 3:5 adds that the earth was formed out of water and by water.
  - See also Psalm 24:2 and Psalm 136:6.
- The Bible appears clear; water was first…and then land. It would be rude to suggest otherwise. But Houston, we have a problem…and it's seriously huge.
  - Job 38:4-11, Psalms 104:5-9, and Proverbs 8:23-30 claim it's the other way around, that is, sea first, and land afterward. This contrary position would, of course, completely refute what had seemed to be an unassailable truth.
  - What does Job 38 say?
    - Job 38:4-6 says that the foundations were first created. Classically foundations refer to something solid, not liquid.
    - This understanding is reinforced in verses 8-11: "Or who enclosed the sea with doors When, bursting forth, it went out from the womb; When I made a cloud its garment And thick darkness its swaddling band, And I placed boundaries on it And set a bolt and doors, And I said, 'Thus far you shall come, but no farther; And here shall your proud waves stop?"
    - Waters burst out from the womb. Human physiology dictates that the womb always precedes the "waters" surrounding a baby. Here too, the womb representing land precedes the

[145]

presentation of the waters, identified in verse 8 as the seas.

- o Psalm 104:5-9
  - Verse 5 affirms that the foundations were first, i.e. land.
  - Then after the "spring of the deep" erupts (Job 38) the waters "covered it (the land) with the deep as with a garment; The waters were standing above the mountains/hills" (Psalm 104:6).
  - This super ocean covered the entire earth verse (Psalm 104:9).
  - The continents and separate oceans are created when the mountains/hills become seriously large and the sea basins drop (Psalms 104:8-9).
- o Proverbs 8
  - The narrative from Proverbs 8 is much longer but actually affirms the land first, waters second scenario twice, first in reverse order and then in chronological order.
  - Reverse order (later events to earlier):
    - Verse 23 "earliest times to the earth" provides the context.
    - Verse 24a "no depths" refers to no oceans.
    - Verse 24b "springs abounding with water."
      - o In Job 38:8 they burst forth from the "womb" to form the oceans.
      - o These are the "spring of the sea" Job 38:16a.
      - o "Like the deep we cannot enter them as we would normal springs" (Job 38:16b).
    - Verse 25 "before the mountains" refers to mountainous lands; similarly, "before the hills" refers to no hilly land (compare Psalms 104:6).
    - Verse 26 "not yet made the earth and fields, nor the first dust of the world" refers to fielded land and even the first dust of the land.

[146]

- Chronological order (earliest events to later events)
  - Verse 27
    - "Established the heavens." Here established (*kuwn*) refers to the process of setting up creation.
    - "When he inscribed a circle on the face of the deep"
      - The Hebrew words here for "face of the deep" are identical to verse 2 of Genesis translated "surface of the deep."
      - From previous discussions of *tohu wa bohu* and from things invisible these would represent the primeval particles.
      - Notice that the inscription of the "circle" comes after the surface of the deep, and not before as suggested by Seven Day creationists.
      - The "circle" represents the waters below (primeval gases) which become the earth (compare Genesis 1:7 and Isaiah 40:22).
  - Verse 28
    - "Made firm the *shachaq* above" (*shachaq* dust, cloud). Making dust solid/hard (*'amats* Hebrew) and not skies makes far better sense (compare Isaiah 40:15). Furthermore, the dust is *min* (of material from which something is made) again supporting dust and not skies as the correct translation.
    - "when the springs of the deep become fixed (*'azaz* strong) refers

to "springs" (Job 38:8) which would "burst forth" creating "seas."

- Verse 29
  - Then continents and separate oceans are created "when he set for the sea" its boundary."
  - The continents: "...when He marked out the foundations of the earth."

- So now at last, we know at last...all three passages (together with Genesis 2), when understood properly, tell us it was the land...and then seas.

But what about the "waters above" and the "waters below"?

- This is clarified by 2 Peter 3:5 and Hebrews 11:3 (see Appendix A).

  "By faith we understand that the worlds were prepared by the word of God, so that what is seen was not made out of things which are visible" (Hebrews 11:3).

  "For when they maintain this, it escapes their notice that by the word of God the heavens existed long ago and the earth was formed out of water and by water..." (2 Peter 3:5).

- The world was made both out of things "not visible" and "out of water"
  - This echoes Genesis 1:2
    - Invisible: (*tohu wa bohu*)
    - Water (particles): Strong's Concordance describes "the surface of the deep" as primeval waters (other scripture uses "water" to describe gaseous particles)
  - The Spirit moves over these invisible waters, compressing the particles into a singularity
  - God commands the singularity to explode ("let there be light")

[148]

- This explosion (Big Bang) produces "waters above and below" representing the <u>invisible waters</u> of the early universe which create our earth and the cosmos
- The <u>only</u> explanation which harmonizes all six passages (Psalm 24:2, Psalm 136:6, Job 38, Proverbs 8, Hebrews 11:3, and 2 Peter 3:5).
- The <u>only</u> argument which preserves the sense of *tohu wa bohu* as empty space and the "surface of the deep" as primeval gases.

Appendix D: Both or Neither

Like many of you I was brought up believing in the Seven Day arguments. This probably explains my sentimental attachments to their camp. While scientists are dismissive of their claims, many fine Christian scholars (including Dr. Terry Mortenson from Answers in Genesis and Dr. Gunn, the linguist who reviewed my Hebrew/Greek) speak with erudition from this perspective. Later in college I was exposed to the Old Earth Creationists who, influenced by the Intelligent Design Movement, believe that the seven days of creation refer to seven immensely long periods of time. Scientists' condescension toward them is ironic, given the evolutionists' addiction to just-so storytelling.

That being said, you may think that you know which side of the age issue, "Seven Day Creationist" or "Old Earthers" I am pursuing.

My answer: Both…or neither. Just not the way that they are presented.

APPENDIX E: Bunnies and Animal Death

> Then God said…"Let the waters teem with swarms of living creatures…"Be fruitful and multiply, and fill the waters in the seas, and let birds multiply on the earth."…"Let the earth bring forth living creatures…Be fruitful and multiply, and fill the earth." (Genesis 1:24-26)

So we did. Together we swarmed, bore fruit, multiplied, brought forth, and filled the earth. We were all of us happy to obey. And no one died.

Seven Day Creationists believe that animal death before Adam's sin would violate both scripture (Romans 8:19-25) and God's integrity. Death was a result of sin, and before the Fall, there wasn't any sin. No exceptions, not for accidental deaths or old age or death by other animals. If there were, then that would mean that God was okay with animal death even before sin. That would be a real problem. This probably strikes you as ridiculous though, because the Garden of Eden was a paradise. Well, a paradise doesn't have problems, that's why it's called a paradise.

But if there really were no animal deaths, a strange predicament arises. All the animals that couldn't die through accidental deaths or old age or by other animals would start to overpopulate the Garden of Eden. It may seem silly to think about, but we can mathematically predict that a single pair of rabbits and their offspring could produce enough bunnies in 50 years to equal twice the number of protons in the entire universe. Paradise, meet your problem. There's simply no way you could fit that many rabbits on the earth, let alone in the Garden of Eden. Let's take a look.

Let's create a thought experiment using a single breeding rabbit pair prior to the "fall." A single female rabbit can have 1-14 babies per litter, but let's be conservative and say that the average litter size is six. But remember, probably only <u>half</u> of those six babies will be females.

So averaging three females/litter, we can now calculate what our annual bunny population would be without animal death.

Rabbit gestation lasts 28-31 days, and because they are induced ovulators, mother rabbits can be impregnated again within minutes of giving birth. This means that mama could, hypothetically, have one litter per month if she is constantly with a male rabbit.

If our starter bunnies begin reproducing at six months of age, and have babies for fifty years, then by the end of the first year:

One mother rabbit x 3 female babies x 12 months = 36 female babies (plus your original mama makes 37). Let's add the new babies to the reproductive population at the beginning of the following year. At that point, their average age would be six months--the time of their first litter. (This works if you consider this to be averaging the new females' reproductive output.) If—starting at the beginning of Year 2—each of the Year One female rabbits produces an average of 3 female offspring per month, then by the

End of Year 2:

37 mother rabbits x 3 female babies x 12 months = 1,332 female babies (plus your original 37 will equal a total of 1,369 total)

End of Year 3:

1,369 mother rabbits x 3 female babies x 12 months = 49,284 female babies (49,284 + last year's 1,369 = 50,653 total)

End of Year 4:

50,653 x 3 x 12 months = 1,823,508 female babies (1,823,508 + last year's 50,653 = 1,874,161 total)

End of Year 5:

1,874,161 x 3 x 12 months = 67,469,796 female babies (67,469,796 + last year's 1,874,161 = 69,343,957 total)

[152]

End of Year 6:

   69,343,957 x 3 x 12 months + last years = 2,565,726,409 female babies

End of Year 7

   94,931,877,133 female babies

Year:

   8: 3,512,479,453,921

   9: 129,961,739,795,077

   10: 4,808,584,372,417,849

   11: 1.779×10 to the 17th

   12: 6.583×10 to the 18th

   13: 2.436×10 to the 20th

   14: 9.012×10 to the 21st

   15: 3.334×10 to the 23rd

   16: 1.234×10 to the 25th

   17: 4.565×10 to the 26th

   18: 1.689×10 to the 28th

   19: 6.249×10 to the 29th

   20: 2.31×10 to the 31st

21: 8.555×10^{32}

22: 3.165×10^{34}

23: 1.171×10^{36}

24: 4.333×10^{37}

25: 1.60×10^{39}

26: 5.933×10^{40}

27: 2.195×10^{42}

28: 8.121×10^{43}

29: 3.005×10^{45}

30: 4.114×10^{48}

31: 1.522×10^{50}

32: 5.632×10^{51}

33: 2.084×10^{53}

34: 7.710×10^{54}

35: 2.853×10^{56}

36: 1.056×10^{58}

37: 3.905×10^{59}

38: 1.445×10^{61}

39: 5.346×10^{62}

40: 1.978×10^{64}

41: 7.319×10^{65}

42: 2.708×10 to the 67th

43: 1.002×10 to the 69th

44: 3.707×10 to the 70th

45: 1.372×10 to the 72nd

46: 5.076×10 to the 73rd

47: 1.878×10 to the 75th

48: 6.948×10 to the 76th

49: 2.571×10 to the 78th

50: 9.512×10 to the 79th

Recall that male offspring will nearly approximate the number of female babies. Together they would number 1.902×10 to the 80th rabbits (1/5th sexvigintillion), twice the estimated number of protons of the entire universe.

Said another way, if we took these rabbits, multiplied by 15 X 15 X 35.5cm (the average size of a medium rabbit), convert to cubic meters, we arrive at a volume of bunnies <u>one thousand trillion times the size of the entire milky way galaxy,</u> a galaxy so wide that if you were traveling at the speed of light it would take 100,000 years just to cross it.

And all that in <u>only</u> 50 years from a single breeding pair of rabbits.

I wonder…just where is Adam going to put all those bunnies? Or did God put Adam and Eve in the garden <u>expecting</u> them to sin right away so other animals could start eating the rabbits?

This, of course, isn't completely fair. Many other things could affect this number. <u>But</u> that would require changing the starting conditions, something the traditionalists are reluctant to do…because it would involve animal death.

A SDC Christian apologist, one whom I respect, told me that anything other than instantaneous creation would require that animals die. He explained that animal death prior to Adam's sin would violate Romans 8:20.

> "For the creation was subjected to futility, not willingly, but because of Him who subjected it, in hope that the creation itself also will be set free from its slavery to corruption (*phthora*) into the freedom of the glory of the children of God."

The word "corruption" is taken from the Greek word, *phthora* (Strongs 5356) meaning: corruption, destruction, perishing; that which is subject to corruption, what is perishable; in the Christian sense, eternal misery in hell; in the NT, in an ethical sense, corruption i.e. moral decay.

My friend's position is that when Adam sinned, all creation (animals) became "enslaved" to *phthora*, that is, they would now die (compare 1 Corinthians 15:42).

As we consider his claim, let me say that it is all based upon conjecture. We know that there were only two times that animal deaths were recorded after Adam's sin. The first is when God performs the first sacrifice, covering Adam's sin with an offering and his and Eve's bodies with skin. The second is that of Abel's sacrifice. There are no further animal deaths recorded in Genesis until the flood (Genesis 7:21-22) over 1600 years later. After the flood receded, God gives man permission for the first time to both kill and eat the animals for food (Genesis 9:3).

All this being so, it turns out that my friend's rendering of Romans 8:20 is really just his opinion. Moreover, it disregards 2 Peter 2:12, the only other time that the Greek work *phthora* is used together with animals in the Bible: "But these (false prophets), like unreasoning animals, born as creatures of instinct to be captured and killed (*phthora*), reviling where they have no knowledge, will in the destruction of those creatures also be destroyed."

Prior to Adam's sin, we have no reason to believe that animals were dangerous. According to Genesis 1:30, they may even have been vegetarians (implied but not explicitly said). But more significantly they were not captured and killed by humans. But after Adam sinned, this all changed. At least some animals became "unreasoning…creatures of instinct." The inference is that they had become dangerous. Therefore they had to be "captured and killed" (*phthora*), more specifically they had to be captured and killed <u>by people</u> (2 Peter 2:12).

The verses in Romans 8:20 and 2 Peter 2:12 complement one another. In 2 Peter 2:12, we see a world changed by sin, a world described in Romans 8:20 as one of futility (*mataiotes*), "perverseness and depravity." The peace was lost between animals and men. The animals were now dangerous, "unreasoning…creatures of instinct." Their relationship to man became one of being…"captured and killed." Animal death now <u>came at the hands of mankind</u>.

This estrangement between animals and mankind will only be resolved with the New Heavens and the New Earth when: "…the wolf will dwell with the lamb, And the leopard will lie down with the young goat, And the calf and the young lion and the fatling together; And a little boy will lead them" (Isaiah 11:6).

In 2 Peter 2:12, *phthora* does describe animal death, but <u>only</u> animal death which comes <u>at the hands of mankind</u>. This understanding is explicit, not inferential. Moreover, this passage is the only one outside of Romans 8:20 which uses *phthora* together with animals.

The insight gained from 2 Peter 2:12 means that there are now at least two explanations for *phthora* in Romans 8:20. Consequently insistence that animals didn't die (from accidents, senescence, or by other animals) prior to Adam's sin is conjectural.

Moreover, if we apply the understanding of *phthora* found in 2 Peter 2:12 to Romans 8:20 we discover that animals could die before man's original sin, just not from man's hand.

Ironically this is often where well-meaning young earth creationists quote evolutionists who pontificate that if God meant for animals to eat each other, then He "certainly (is) not the sort of God to whom anyone would be inclined to pray." Other adjectives used to describe this type of God are "evil," "blind," "cruel," and "dreadful ethical."

But before presuming to tell God how He should behave they should consider passage in Psalms. "The young lions roar after their prey And seek their food from God" (Psalms 104:21).

Commenting on this verse, the psalmist adds: "Let the glory of the LORD endure forever; Let the LORD be glad in His works" (Psalms 104:31).

Also consider Job 38:4, 39-40. Verse 4 says: "Where were you when I laid the foundation of the earth? Tell Me, if you have understanding." Verses 39-40 add: "Can you hunt the prey for the lion, Or satisfy the appetite of the young lions, When they crouch in their dens And lie in wait in their lair?"

The point is that we need to exercise humility in exegesis. So as we look at Genesis 1:30 (God provides green plants for food) we must remember to balance that against Psalm 104:21 and Job 38:39.

APPENDIX F: God's Clock and Man's Unrest

Day seven offers us another look at God's Clock.

> "Thus the heavens and the earth were completed, and all their hosts. By the seventh day God completed His work which He had done, and He rested on the seventh day from all His work which He had done. Then God blessed the seventh day and sanctified it, because in it He rested from all His work which God had created and made" (Genesis 2:1-3).

Pretty straightforward. The work is done, time to relax, put up your feet and rest. But then, a twist. God rests on the seventh day. Others don't: "For we who have believed enter that rest, just as He has said, **as I swore in my wrath, they shall not enter my rest**," although His works were finished from the foundation of the world" (Hebrews 4:3, also 4:4-11; bold emphasis mine).

The Pulpit Commentary explains that God's rest "had been from the beginning, and man had not yet entered into it…"

Clearly there are two very different clocks measuring two very different kinds of days. First, we see God's Clock representing God's Days in Hebrews 4:4: "And God rested on the seventh day from all His works" (see also Genesis 2:1-3). Second, we have Man's Clock representing Man's (24 hour rotatory) days: "Since it remains for some to enter it [the rest]…He again fixes a certain day, 'Today'" (Hebrews 4:7, see also Psalm 95:8-11).

While some say the text in Hebrews 4:7 is metaphorical it is clearly literal in Psalm 95:8-11.

> Today, if you would hear His voice, Do not harden your hearts, as at Meribah, As in the day of Massah in the wilderness, 'When your fathers tested Me, They tried Me, though they had seen My work.' 'For forty years I loathed that generation, And said they are a people who

err in their heart, And they do not know My ways.'
'Therefore I swore in My anger, Truly they shall not
enter into My rest.'

Both descriptions describe day seven as continuing unabated for
thousands of man's years. It's clear that many have still not entered
God's rest. From this we can say too things. First, it unquestionably
confirms the idea of two very different kinds of clocks in Genesis, man's
and God's. And second, day seven <u>has</u> to represent God's clock, not a
literal 24-hour rotatory man's day. This use of God's Clock is supported
by a study Hebrews 4:4-11 together with Genesis 2:1-3.

But some SDC apologists say that this is because Day Seven is
described without an evening or a morning. Maybe so, but even if you
don't describe the evening and morning for man's days they still only
last 24 hours.

This might also be a good time to pause and clarify some points I
made previously. God's Clock/Days are used to number all seven days
of the Creation Week. But the sixth day is special because at the end of
this day is when man was created and his clock begins. That being the
case, you might wonder why Moses didn't switch to Man's Clock when
that happened. Certainly Moses could have done that. But let's look at
other scriptures to see how this is handled.

We see God's Clock being used in both Testaments. Daniel uses
it to describe the last days. The Minor Prophets use it to characterize
"the day of the Lord." It's even used immediately after the Creation
Week (Genesis 2:17) when God warns Adam that should he eat from the
tree of the knowledge of good and evil, he will die on that very "day."
But Adam doesn't die in the next 24 hours. In fact, he continues to live
more than 800 additional years (Genesis 5:4). The only way for him to
die on the same day is use God's Clock, with the day Adam died
consisting of a vastly extended period of time (see discussion on Psalms
90 in Chapter Three).

From these passages we are able to make three general
comments. First, God's Clock is often used when the Bible describes
significant events. Second, in all of those descriptions, God's and Man's

Clock are running side by side (compare Psalm 90:4-6 and 2nd Peter 3:8). Finally, while God's Clock may be compared to Man's Clock, the author is not compelled to switch back and forth except to provide clarity.

Moses' use of God's Clock is perfectly consistent with how God's Clock is handled elsewhere in the Bible. His use of God's Clock to describe all seven days emphasizes creation events rather than the time period. He isn't compelled to switch back and forth between God's and Man's Clocks. As in other passages, usage of God's Clock is not changed even when Man's Clock begins because the usage is unaffected even when both clocks are running simultaneously. That last point is true even if Man's Clock had begun on day one. And as in other passages, God's Clock in Genesis can be seen to explain nuances from God's perspective as well as man's.

Appendix G: TIMING is EVERYTHING

- Hebrews 11: 3 has one more thing to tell us:

  > By faith we understand that the worlds were prepared by the word of God, so that what is seen was not made out of things which are visible (Hebrews 11:3).

- There's no nice way to say this. The translation has been tampered with.
- The word translated "worlds" comes from *aion* (Gr). It's where we get the transliteration "eon(s)" in English.
- *Aion* is used 95 times in the Bible and all but eight have to do with ages, eons.
- Seven times *aion* is translated "world."
- Changing those seven times from "world" to "age(s)" changes nothing in the meaning.
- Only Hebrews 11:3 has the meaning changed by using "worlds" instead of "eon(s)."
- 16 dictionaries/lexicons below <u>always</u> translate *aeon* as "ages," "eons," etc.[clxvi]
- So why translate *aions* in Hebrews 11:3 as "worlds"?
- I can only think to reduce the embarrassment of those who insist on 24 hour days.
- A proper translation would require them to explain why creation "days" involve "eons" of time.

  > "By faith we understand that the <u>eons</u> were prepared by the word of God, so that what is seen was not made out of things which are visible" (Hebrews 11:3).

Appendix H: 199 REASONS TO BELIEVE

1. There are fewer than 9,000 Hebrew words in the Old Testament.[1] Many words (i.e. heaven, *shamayim*) express multiple meanings which are understood contextually.
2. Moses had to use language accessible to an audience which was scientifically unsophisticated.
3. Moses describes evenings and mornings for the first three days even though the earth and sun were not created until the third and fourth day, respectively.
4. The Bible has five creation accounts (Genesis 1-2, Job 38, Proverbs 8, Psalms 104) which help to specify the order of creation.
5. Moses, the author of Genesis, wrote a primer in Psalm 90 to explain the language in Genesis.
6. Outside of these passages are over 200 additional verses which amplify our understanding of creation.

Evening/Morning and Seven Day Creationists

7. SDCs claim that the earth was created on the first day (Genesis 1:2).
8. Proverbs 8:27 rejects this because the earth was made after and not before the deep.
9. *Tohu wa bohu* in Genesis 1: 2 should be translated "nothingness" and "empty space" and "emptiness".
10. But most English Bible versions translate *tohu wa bohu* in Genesis 1: 2 as "formless and void".
11. Translating *tohu wa bohu* in such an obscure way ("formless and void") allows commentaries to say that this meant that the earth was a wasteland.
12. But Isaiah 45:18 specifically addresses creation and says that God did not create a wasteland (*tohu*).
13. The proper translation of *tohu* in Genesis 1:2 as "nothingness" and "empty space" is consistent with how *tohu* is translated in Job 6:18 (nothing).

---

[1] Blair Lasfeldt, Biblical Hebrew Made Easy!

14. The proper translation of *tohu* in Genesis 1:2 as "nothingness" and "empty space" is consistent with how *tohu* is translated in Job 26:7 (nothing).

15. The proper translation of *tohu* in Genesis 1:2 as "nothingness" and "empty space" is consistent with how it is *tohu* is translated in Isaiah 41:29 (emptiness).

16. The proper translation of *tohu* in Genesis 1:2 as "nothingness" and "empty space" is consistent with how it is *tohu* is translated in Isaiah 49:4 (nothing).

17. The proper translation of *bohuw* in Genesis 1:2 as "emptiness" follows the way *bohuw* is translated in Isaiah 34:11 (emptiness).

18. Jewish scholars who were commissioned two centuries before Christ to translate their native language of Hebrew into Greek agreed; translating *tohu* and *bohu* as *aoratos*, "invisible" and *akataskeuastos*, "unprepared."[2]

19. The timeline in reverse order (Proverbs 8:23-26 together with Job 38:8 and Genesis 1:9-10) rejects SDC claims of the earth on Day One.

20. The timeline in chronological order (Proverbs 8:27-30) rejects SDC claims of the earth on Day One.

21. The SDCs claim that the first three days without a sun were rotatory is conjectural and without scriptural support.

22. SDCs "rotatory days" have no sun for the necessary sunset and sunrise each evening and morning.

23. The Bible says sun needed for sunrise/sunset for morning/evening (Mark 1:32, 2 Samuel 23:4).

24. Genesis 1:14-15, 17 all reference the "expanse" as universe, not atmosphere as SDCs claim.

25. Job 38:9 (compare with Genesis 1:9-10) specifically describes the creation of the atmosphere on day three, no day two as SDCs claim.

Evening/morning and Old Earthers

26. OEs claim Genesis 1:1 describes creation of universe ("Heaven and earth" (*hashamayim we ha 'erets)*.

---

[2] Footnote: Alfred Rahlfs, ed., *Septuaginta*, 7th ed. (Stutgart: Wurtenbergische Bibelanstalt, 1962.

27. OEs claim that this would mean that the sun was created prior to the seven days of creation.

28. OEs claim that days of creation only describe function from man's point of view and happened after Genesis 1:1.

29. OEs claim this is supported by the use of "made" (`asah) rather than "create" (`asah) in verse 17 actually damage their argument and favor God's Clock (i.e. star formation).

30. Genesis 2:1-2, 4 and Exodus 20:11 contradict the notion that the Creation Week only describes function and not creation.

31. Genesis 1:9-10 rejects the notion the earth was created prior to day three.

32. Genesis 1:16-17 reject the OE claim that the sun was created prior to the creation week.

Evening/morning and God's Clock

33. God's Clock is used to number the Creation Week; Man's Clock doesn't begin until man was created toward the end of Day Six.

34. God's Clock is found in Genesis 2:17 ("in the day (God's day) you eat that you will surely die" after which Adam lived for hundreds of years (man's days). Isaiah 13:6, 9, Lamentations 2:22, Daniel 7:25, 9:24-27, 12:1-7, Ezekiel 13:5, 30:3, Joel 1:15, 2:1, 11, 2:31, 3:14, Amos 5:18, 20, Obadiah 1:15, Zephaniah 1:7,8, 14, 18, 2:2-3 Malachi 4:5, Luke, Acts 2:20, Romans 13:12, 1 Corinthians 5:5, 1 Thessalonians 5:1-2, 2 Thessalonians 2:2, Hebrews 1:2, 1:5, 4:3-11, 10:25, 37, James 5:8, 1 Peter 4:7, 2 Peter 2:9, 3:10, 1 John 2:18 (it is the last hour), Jude 1:25 (before man's time) and Revelation 11:3, 5, 12:6, 14.

    Also when the Bible says: "the day is near" Ezekiel 30:3, Romans 13:12, Isaiah 13:6, Joel 1:15, 2:1, 3:14, Zephaniah 1:7, Romans 13:11-12, James 5:8, 1 Peter 4:7, Revelation 1:3, 22:10.

35. God and man's clocks are compared mathematically: compare Daniel 12:1-7 with verses 11-12, also 8:14, Revelation 11:3, 13:5 compare Revelation 12:6 and 12:14.

36. The Bible uses God's Clock to describe significant events ("the day of the Lord," the Second Coming, etc.).

37. Because God's Clock and Man's Clock run simultaneously, all my points remain valid even if Man's Clock had actually begun on day one.
38. Using God's Clock in Genesis employs elements of both SDCs and OEs and is consistent with scripture.
39. When Moses wrote Psalm 90, he created four similes which unlock the language in Genesis.
40. Psalms 90:4a explains that in God's clock, days consist of eons of time from man's perspective.
41. Psalms 90:4b explains that in God's clock, days can have variable lengths from man's perspective.
42. Psalms 90:6 uses the same words for "evening" and "morning" to mean "beginning" and "end."
43. But translating *erev* and *boqer* as "evening" and "morning" rather than "beginning" and "end" would change nothing because these are the extremes of God's days.
44. The Hebrew word *yom* also means extended periods of time.
45. SDC's argument that numbering *yom* means these are 24 hour days is not supported because these are God's day one, two, and so on.
46. Using God's clock in Genesis, *yom* would be variable and consist of eons of time.
47. Hebrews 11:3 confirms that Genesis used God's clock with eons of time.
48. Not seen in modern English translations because *aion* (Gk) in Hebrews 11:3 is changed from the transliterated English word "eon(s)" to the SDC acceptable "worlds" (see Appendix G, Timing is Everything).
49. God's Clock is consistent with OT references to the creation week, (i.e. Exodus 20:11).
50. God's Clock is consistent with quotes by Jesus regarding the creation week.
51. "Time dilation," (the idea that time slows down as one approaches the speed of light) merely helps us understand but is not necessary for the validity of "God's Clock."
52. Using God's Days (variable vastly extended periods of time) together with overlapping days resolves evening/morning problems.

Particles and Space (God's Clock)

53. God began to "set up" the universe on day one (Genesis 1:2, Proverb 8:27, 28).

54. The "unformed empty space" *tohu wa bohu* (verse 2) is consistent with God's Clock and represents particles God uses as building blocks to fashion the earth (see the merism in Genesis 1:1, use of tohu in Job 26:7).

55. In God's Clock, the surface of the waters in Genesis 1:2 would refer to gas particles.

56. Precedent exists for this since the Bible has used water to describe gases on three other occasions (Job 26:8; 2 Samuel 22:12; Psalms 18:11).

57. Primordial particles are confirmed in Hebrews 11:3 and 2 Peter 3:5, whereby the "word of God" placed together the world with "not visible" "waters" (primordial gases).

58. Hebrews 11:3b amplifies verse 1 which recalls "things" hoped for and "conviction of things" not seen, never things hoped for and conviction in things that didn't even exist.

59. Consequently, Hebrews 11:3b (what is seen was not made out of things which are visible) cannot refer to *ex nihilo*.

60. There are over 100 examples in Hebrews 11, all of which refer to things which exist but just cannot be seen, never non-existent things which cannot be seen.

61. Between Hebrews 11a citing "eons" of time and Hebrews 11b giving support for primordial particles we have confirmation of God's clock and the particles anticipating the birth of the universe.

Light and Seven Day Creationists

62. The light in Genesis 1:3 cannot be the sun, moon, or stars which were not created until the fourth day (Genesis 1:17).

63. The light in Genesis 1:3-4 cannot be the illumination from the glory of God as described in Revelation 21:25 because that light has no night as is explicitly required by Genesis 1:4.

64. Seven Day Creationists can only speculate what this light might have been or how it caused day and night.

Light and Old Earthers

65. Genesis 1:10, 16 contradicts the OE claim that the sun preceded the earth.
66. OEs claim the light in Genesis 1:3 is the sun which penetrates the clouds on the fourth day (Job 38:9).
67. A careful reading of the context of Job 38 together with Genesis 1:9-10 reveals that this thick cloud was not present until day three.
68. That means that no cloud would have been blocking the sun on days one and two if, in fact, the sun had been created prior to the Creation Week.
69. We are told in Genesis that only a fully developed sun can separate day and night (Genesis 1:14-18).
70. Without a sun the OE would have no explanation for night (Genesis 1:5).

Light and God's Clock

71. Using God's Clock, the light in Genesis 1:3 represents the explosive power of the Big Bang.
72. According to an MIT physics professor, Genesis 1 follows the scientific description of the Big Bang exactly.
73. God saw that the light was good/*towb* (Genesis 1:4). *Towb* translated "good" suggests a design component, deemed necessary by cosmologists for life.
74. *Yowm* (Strongs 03117) translated "day") in Genesis 1:5 also means "time."
75. Genesis 1:5 records the creation of time and matter together.
76. Simultaneous creation of "time" and "matter" fits scientific understandings.
77. God used Big Bang's explosive to create an expanse, "stretching" the universe (Isaiah 42:5, 51:13, Jeremiah 10:12).
78. In Genesis 1:5 *choshek* is called *layil* ("night" also rendered "protective shadow").
79. Job 38:19-20 also refer to darkness/*chosek* as a physical space.
80. *Ben badal* in Genesis 1:5 literally means to "divide a physical space," in this case between light and dark.
81. Suggests that darkness is a physical space (although it can also be used otherwise).
82. "Obscurity" and "protective shadow" easily describe those regions surrounding the universe beyond the Big Bang.

83. Seven Day Creationists and some Old Earthers both believe that the heavens described in Genesis 1:8 represent the earth's atmosphere.

84. This is based upon biblical support for three heavens: 1) the earth's atmosphere; 2) the universe excepting the earth; and 3) God's throne room.

85. Mislabeling heaven in Genesis 1:8 as earth's atmosphere ignores Genesis 1:14-15, 17) in which the expanse/heaven refers to the entire universe excepting the earth.

86. It is rejected by Proverbs 8:24-26 (together with Genesis 1:9-10) which describe the same events in reverse order.

87. It is rejected by Proverbs 8:27-28 (together with Job 38:8-9) describing early creation days in chronological order.

88. It is rejected by the discussion of the deep, circle on the deep, cosmic explosion producing waters above and below which were not visible.

89. It ignores the consequence of a sunless earth (no source of heat, photosynthesis) for 24 hours.

90. It is rejected by Job 38:9 which records the creation of atmosphere on day three.

91. Ignores the consequences of absent atmosphere necessary to diffuse and retain solar heat as well as shield the earth from deadly radiation (Job 38:9).

Rain

92. The SDC concept that it never rained prior to the flood is specifically negated in Genesis 3:17 which discusses "plants of the field."

93. According to the conditions in Genesis 2:5 "plants of the field" would require both man and rain.

94. Moreover, God's declaration in Genesis 1:29 gives Adam and Eve "every plant yielding seed."

95. The Hebrew word, `eseb translated as plant in Genesis 1:29 is the same word translated as plant from Genesis 2:5.

96. Comparing Genesis 1:27 (day six and the creation of Adam and Eve) with Genesis 2:7-23 we know that the Garden of Eden was created on day six.

97. These four passages Genesis 1:27, 29, Genesis 2:5 and Genesis 2:7-23 indicate that rain probably also had to occur in the Garden of Eden.
98. Since it absolutely rained (man's judgment for sin, Garden of Eden as above) it is unlikely that the "waters above" represent a canopy which was emptied at the time of the flood.

The Heavens and God's Clock

99. The heaven described in Genesis 1:8 can only be the universe excepting the earth.
100. Genesis 1:17 explains that this heaven is where God places the sun and moon and stars.
101. The "water above" from the Hebrew *min al* suggests that these "waters" were "of material above (or against) from which something is made, as a source or origin."
102. The "waters above (against)" the expanse called heaven (our universe) then represents the unformed building blocks of the universe.
103. Meanwhile the "waters below," *min tachath*, were "of material below from which something is made, as a source or origin."
104. The "waters below" the expanse called heaven (our universe) then represents the unformed building blocks of particles being set aside for the construction of the earth.
105. But the capper is that God Himself declares that the earth was made on Day Three when the dry land appeared (Genesis 1:10).
106. Recall that this understanding is reinforced when comparing Hebrews 11:3 with 2 Peter 3:5.

Temperature and Seven Day Creationists

107. SDCs have a temperature problem. Day three would be a chilly 454.5°F below zero, freezing any vegetation in minutes.
108. Cannot appeal to the sun or stars since they were not created until Day Four (Genesis 1:16-19).
109. Cannot appeal to the "glory of God" as in Revelation 21:25 since that light had no night.
110. Amplified by absence of atmosphere, not present until day three (Job 38:9) necessary to shield lethal radiation and for solar heat to heat correctly.

Temperature and Old Earthers

111. OEs share the same temperature and atmosphere problem. We've already explained how they can't appeal to the sun for a heat source.

Temperature, Overlapping Days, and God's Clock

112. The temperature problem is a reflection of misreading of Genesis which clearly supports overlapping days.
113. Overlapping days explains why plants can continue to sprout from Day Three until the sixth day (Genesis 1:11, 2:5).
114. That these plants were present in the Garden of Eden is supported by Genesis 1:29 which uses the same Hebrew word, `eseb for "plants" as in Genesis 2:5.
115. Overlapping days prevents plants from freezing solid.
116. Overlapping days can explain the order of plants and animals.
117. Overlapping days can explain the sun and photosynthesis.
118. Overlapping days can explain the relative ages of the earth and universe.
119. The variances between scientific findings and God's Clock are either eliminated or inconsequential with "overlapping days."
120. Compare overlapping days to a cook with six tasks. Task one begins before task two which begins before task three and so on. But task one can also continue after task two or three have already begun.

The Chicken and the Egg

121. Genesis 1:6-9 uses "waters" to say primordial particles were first.
122. "Let the waters (primordial particles) below the heavens be gathered into one place, and let the dry land appear (land first)"
123. The idea of primordial particles is affirmed by 2 Peter 3:5 and Hebrews 11:3.
124. Understanding "waters" as primordial particles is strengthened by Proverbs 8:28.
125. Proverbs 8:28 makes more sense translated "When He made firm the *dust* above (consistent with Strong's Number 07834).

126. Shouldn't bother Christians that Moses speaking to a non-scientific audience uses "waters" in Genesis 1:9 to refer to primordial particles.
127. Using "waters" and "deep" in different ways shouldn't bother Christians who use "heavens" in three different ways.
128. SDC teaching that the oceans were created before the land is not consistent with ALL scripture.
129. Job 38:4-6 and 8-11 suggest that the land was created first.
130. Psalms 104:5 affirms that foundation, i.e. land was first.
131. Proverbs 8:24-26 agrees (in reverse order) that the land was created first.
132. Proverbs 8:28,-29 agrees (chronological order) that the land was created first.
133. Job 38:8, 16 suggest the fountains of the deep (springs of the sea) were created after the land.
134. Proverbs 8:28 (chronological order) agrees that the earth (dust was made firm) was made prior to the springs of the deep becoming fixed.
135. Proverbs 8:24 (reverse order) says the springs of the deep preceded the oceans (depths).
136. Job 38:8 agree the springs "bursting forth" created the seas.
137. Psalm 104:6, 9 describe water forming a deep which covers then covers the earth.
138. Psalm 104:8-9 describe continents and separate oceans as the mountains rise and the sea beds drop.

Animal Death and Seven Day Creationists

139. SDCs use Romans 8:21 to claim that animal death (*phthora*) is a result of man's sin and will be resolved in the "last times."
140. SDCs claim non-possibility of animal death prior to Adam's sin precludes natural selection as a process to effect "change after their kind".
141. Second Peter 2:12, the only other verse with *phthora* and animal death, explicitly teaches that (*phthora*) related to animal death is death that comes at the hands of mankind (2 Peter 2:12).
142. This means that Romans 8:21 now has two possible explanations for animal death: animals dying prior to Adam's sin (of old age or being eaten) OR man killing animals after Adam's sin.

143. Consequently, choosing one of these over the other is conjectural and must be balanced against other scripture.
144. Without animal death a single amorous pair of rabbits could wreak havoc in an incredibly short period of time.
145. These bunnies would fill the entire Milky Way over 1000 trillion times in 50 years.
146. Both Job 38 and Psalm 104 teach that God glories in the lion's predation of other animals.
147. People should be cautious when calling God evil if He is glad in His works, including lion predation (Psalm 104:21, 31).

Natural Selection and All Three

148. Natural selection is used by "Seven Day Creationists," "Old Earthers," and God's Clock.
149. The difference is at which particular taxa each group believes that it takes place.

After Their Kind and All Three

150. All change "after their kind" (Genesis 1:11, 21, 24) can be affected by Natural Selection (i.e. animal breeding, etc.)
151. Translating "kind" as species must be tempered by the fact that the word species is never once used in the Bible.
152. Moreover, scientists today have proposed over 2 dozen definitions for species.
153. Note that "kind" is used differently in the Bible when referring to specific animals or groups of unlike animals.
154. The key is that biblical change happens at God's command (Genesis 1:11, 21, 24).
155. The particular taxa at which natural selection happens is under dispute between "Seven Day Creationists," "Old Earthers," and God's Clock.

Day Seven

156. Day seven is an unusual day and discussion would exceed the scope of this chapter (see Appendix F).
157. Suffice it to say that day seven clearly records God's activity of resting.

158. God's rest together with a careful reading of Hebrews 4:4-7 (see text) reveal that day seven is not a literal 24-hour day but from man's perspective would represent 1000s of years.
159. Some say day seven only has an "appearance" of lasting over 24 hours, anything else is simply metaphorical.
160. That position is clearly refuted by Psalm 95:7-11 which describes some of the Jews at Meribah and Massah which did not enter God's rest for 40 years.
161. This extended period of time in Day Seven would be totally consistent with God's Clock.

My Opinion

162. Natural Selection is a valid methodology (i.e. animal breeding).
163. Everyone, SDCs, OEs, God's Clock proponents, evolutionists believe in natural selection.
164. Everybody believes that change happens as a result of natural selection.
165. The difference is where natural selection takes place.
166. Bible says change takes place "after their kind."
167. After their "kind" is translated from *miyn*.
168. Most of the church believes this means changes happens with species.
169. *Answers in Genesis* says change happens at the "families/orders" level.
170. The Bible never actually uses the word "species" or Linnaean "family" or "order."
171. When *miyn* is used with single animals, it likely means species.
172. When *miyn* is used with large groups, it probably means members of that group, even possibly phyla/kingdom/domain.
173. OEs say change happens at the level of phylum (category below plant and animal kingdoms).
174. OEs propose a type of theistic evolution, i.e. change happens randomly by chance.
175. Evolutionists say change happens randomly at the level of (plant or animal) kingdom/domain.
176. Every phyla known today has been found in the Burgess Shale from the Cambrian Period

177. Some evolutionists described this event as appearing like "special creation."

178. By this meant that these phyla created all life "after their kind."

179. Using *miyn* at the level of phyla/kingdom/domain is compatible with scripture if used with God's Clock.

180. Using God's Clock with phyla/kingdom/domain is not theistic evolution.

181. Using God's Clock, change at the phyla/kingdom/domain happens at God's command and according to God's laws.

182. Evolutionists attempt to use the method of natural selection to prove they are right.

183. Evolution: Too many animals for all to survive. The fittest survive. They pass on their traits and form new species.

184. Ask: Which one's survived? The fittest. How do you know they were the fittest? They survived.

185. Trying to use this method to prove itself results in a tautology.

186. Tautologies lack verification and falsification.

187. Natural selection is a valid methodology to describe change.

188. Natural selection cannot validate itself.

189. Natural selection must be validated by verification and falsification.

190. Natural selection could describe the method God used to create change in His command for animals to reproduce "after their kind."

191. Change would appear random but still operate according to God's laws and in response to His command.

192. This is analogous to jumping from a plane; no one knows where you will land. It appears random. But because of God's law of gravity you will fall.

193. Using natural selection this way, together with God's Clock, is completely consistent with scripture.

194. God's Clock would mean that there are seven days of creation from His perspective (a variant of SDCs) and seven ages of time from man's point of view (a variant of OEs).

195. Seven Day or Old Earth explanations could still be correct, just not the way they are set up presently.

196. Either SDCs, OEs or as I proposed (God's Clock) have more explanatory force than evolution.

197. Let us avoid arrogance and skepticism. Arrogance: denouncing other Christians as wrong. Skepticism: dismissing Genesis One and Two.
198. The bottom line is that this is God's story, not ours.
199. He has also set eternity in their heart, yet so that man will not find out the work which God has done from the beginning even to the end. No one can claim certainty regarding origins (Ecclesiastes 3:11).

NOTES

INTRODUCTION

[i] In Proverbs 2:6 we learn that God gives wisdom, knowledge, and understanding: "For the LORD gives wisdom; From His mouth come knowledge and understanding." In Proverbs 2:9, we find that He does this so that we can discern justice (and righteousness and equity): ...then you will discern righteousness and justice and equity and every good course."

[ii] *Shama,* שָׁמַע **Strong's Number:** 8085; to hear, listen to, obey.

[iii] While we aren't immediately given wisdom and discernment like Solomon was, we can receive them indirectly by studying Proverbs.

[iv] "The square," short-hand for the "public square," understood to represent both the marketplace of goods (business) and also metaphorically, the marketplace of ideas (education).

[v] "The gates," historically for the Jews, were the site of the law courts and government.

[vi] Other nuances include "young, inexperienced, easily seduced."

[vii] The two words in Pr. 1:21, "scoffers" and "scoffing," are related but distinct terms. The one for "Scoffers" is actually: *Liyts. Latson,* is a related term that is translated "scoffing." *Liyts* also implies the idea of "bragging." (Koehler, Ludwig, Walter Baumgartner, M. E. J. Richardson, and Johann Jakob Stamm. *The Hebrew and Aramaic Lexicon of the Old Testament.* Leiden; New York: E.J. Brill, 1999.)

[viii] *Pethiy,* יְתֶפ **Strong's Number:** 6612; simplicity, naivete adj, simple, foolish, open-minded.

[ix] *Meshuwbah,* הָבוּשְׁמ **Strong's Number:** 4878; turning away, turning back, apostasy, backsliding, apostasies, apostasy, faithless, faithlessness, turning, waywardness

[x] Years ago, before the transfer of power, my wife and I crossed into "white" governed South Africa to buy supplies not available where we lived. While staying at a religious retreat, I was approached by a seminarian, eager to speak to an "American" about the end of white rule. He said:

"I have always respected the black man's right to live and prosper without interference from the whites."

Do you recognize what he was saying? He was giving me a sanitized version of apartheid. I'm afraid my reply wasn't very gracious:

"God never asked you to respect the blacks. He called you to love them. And anyone who says He loves God and hates his brother is a liar" (see 1 John 4:20).

Sadly that was the end of the conversation.

God does not ask us to be open-minded with those in need. He wants us to love them. Love is not simple open-mindedness and respect. It's time...and sweat. It is getting under the load and lending a hand (Galatians 6:1-2).

An example of this is when a homosexual friend had made plans to end his life. Other Christians backed off...with the requisite farewell..."if you need anything." Pithy words of respect. But I spent a year listening to him and loving him gently with God's truth. When he got back on his feet, he offered, and ultimately did write a letter of recommendation for my application to medical school.

xi *Pathah* פָּתָה **Strong's Number:** 6601; to be spacious, be open, be wide, (*Hiphil*) to make spacious, make open to be simple, entice, deceive, persuade, (*Qal*) to be open-minded, be simple, be naïve, to be enticed, be deceived; (*Niphal*) to be deceived, be gullible (*Piel*) to persuade, seduce, to deceive, (*Pual*) to be persuaded, to be deceived.

xii *'ahab*, אָהֵב, **Strong's Number:** 157; human love for another, includes family, and sexual.

CHAPTER 1—He Said, She Said

xiii The following discussion is specific to husbands and wives and will not address all the questions that people may have about women roles in the Bible.

xiv The Greeks had a third voice, the middle voice, in addition to the passive and active voices.

xv *Hupotasso* ὑποτάσσω **Strong's Number:** 5293; In non-military use, it was "a voluntary attitude of giving in, cooperating, assuming responsibility, and carrying a burden."

xvi 1 Thessalonians 5:21.

xvii Recorded by St. Luke in Acts 17:11, compare Luke 1:1-4, Acts 1:1

xviii Dr. Gunn, the scholar reviewing my Greek, explained that my pastors possibly got confused because in Galatians 2:20 *paradidomi* is followed by a reflexive pronoun, i.e. "gave himself." Despite that, it is incorrect to say that these are in the middle voice.

xix See Matthew 21:42; Mark 12:10; Luke 20:17; Acts 4:11, 18:6; 1 Corinthians 11:3-5; Ephesians 1:22, 4:15, 5:23; Colossians 1:18, 2:10, 2:19; and 1 Peter 2:7.

xx *Kefale,* κεφαλή **Strong's Number**: 2776; The head, metaphorically anything supreme, chief, prominent of persons, master lord; of a husband in relation to his wife of Christ; the Lord of the husband and of the Church of things; the corner stone.

xxi For example, the cognate term *kefalaios* (κεφάλαιος) is found in Lucianos (2nd cent. AD) and Julianus Imperator (4th cent. AD) of the head of the philosophers; and the related term *kefalaiotes* (κεφαλαιωτής) refers to "the secretary and treasurer of a group of landowners or artisans, tax-collector, etc.; *kefalergeretes* (κεφαληγερέτης) means "the head collector." And in Hermas, Similitudes 7.3, *kefale* refers to the father as head of the family.

xxii Jonathan Burke has exhaustively reviewed all the Standard professional lexicons in regards to *kephale*. They unanimously reject Dr. Bristow's conclusions and are uniform in defining *kephale* as "pre-eminent status or authority," i.e. chief. His work is redacted to review only the pertinent information.

***

Friberg, Friberg, and Miller

In the *Analytical Lexicon of the Greek New Testament,* Friberg, Friberg, and Miller explain that *kephale* means "of persons, **designating first or superior rank head 1C 11.3.**" (bold emphasis mine)."

Friberg, Timothy, Barbara Friberg, and Neva F. Miller. Analytical Lexicon of the Greek New Testament. Vol. 4. Grand Rapids, MI: Baker,

2000. 229. Print.

Arndt, Danker, and Bauer

In *A Greek-English lexicon of the New Testament and other early Christian literature*, Ardnt, Danker and Bauer explain that *kephale* means: "**In the case of living beings, to denote superior rank** (compare Artem. 4, 24 p. 218, 8 ἡ κ. is the symbol of the father; Judg 11:11; 2 Km 22:44) head (Zosimus of Ashkelon [500 A.D.] hails Demosth **as his master**: ὦ θεία κεφαλή [Biogr. p. 297])" (bold emphasis mine).

Additionally, they say: "...**of the father as head of the family Hs 7, 3; of the husband in relation to his wife 1 Cor 11:3b; Eph 5:23a**" (bold emphasis mine)

Danker, Frederick W., Walter Bauer, and William Arndt. *A Greek-English Lexicon of the New Testament and Other Early Christian Literature*. 3rd ed. Chicago: University of Chicago, 2000. 541. Print.

Balz and Schneider

In the Exegetical dictionary of the New Testament, Balz and Schneider say,

> "**The meaning of κεφαλή as leader, chief, master,** which is attested for the Hebrew and Aramaic equivalents (see also KQT 197f.) and mediated through Hellenistic Judaism (LXX, Philo, T. 12 Patr.), **allows Paul in 1 Cor 11:3 to combine the sociological fact of ancient patriarchalism (Theissen 107f.) with the theological idea of origin and rule**" (Balz & Schneider; bold emphasis mine).

Balz, Horst Robert., and Gerhard Schneider. Exegetical Dictionary of the New Testament: Translation of Exegetisches Worterbuch Zum Neuen Testamen. Vol. 1. Grand Rapids, MI: William B. Eerdmans, 1993. 285. Print.

Louw and Nida

In the *Greek-English lexicon of the New Testament: Based on semantic domains*, Louw and Nida write:

> "87.51 κεφαλή, ῆς : **(a figurative extension of meaning** of κεφαλήα 'head,' 8.10) **one who is of supreme or pre-eminent status, in view of authority to order or command**—'one who is the head of, one who is superior to, one who is supreme over.'
>
> ὅς ἐστιν ἡ κεφαλή, Χριστός 'who is the head, (even) Christ' Eph 4.15; παντὸς ἀνδρὸς ἡ κεφαλὴ ὁ Χριστός ἐστιν, κεφαλὴ δὲ γυναικὸς ὁ ἀνήρ, κεφαλὴ δὲ τοῦ Χριστοῦ ὁ θεός '**Christ is supreme over every man, the husband is supreme over his wife, and God is supreme over Christ 1 Cor. 11:3.**'"
> (bold emphasis mine).

Louw, J. P., and Eugene A. Nida. Greek-English Lexicon of the New Testament: Based on Semantic Domains. Vol. 1. N.p.: n.p., 1989. 738. Print.

Swanson

In the *Dictionary of Biblical Languages with Semantic Domains: Greek (New Testament)*, Swanson writes: "… 2. LN 87.51 **superior, one of pre-eminent status, figurative extension of first entry 1 Cor. 11:3**" (bold emphasis mine).

Swanson. Dictionary of Biblical Languages with Semantic Domains: Greek (New Testament). 2nd ed. Vol. 81. N.p.: Logos Research Systems, 2001. Print.

Kittel, Bromily, and Friedrich

In the *Theological dictionary of the New Testament*, Kittel, Bromily, and Friedrich say:

2. **In 1 Cor. 11:3**, in relation to the question of the veiling of women in divine service, Paul says: θέλω δὲ ὑμᾶς εἰδέναι, ὅτι παντὸς ἀνδρὸς ἡ κεφαλὴ ὁ Χριστός ἐστιν, κεφαλὴ δὲ γυναικὸς ὁ ἀνήρ, κεφαλὴ δὲ τοῦ Χριστοῦ ὁ θεός. From 11:7: ἀνὴρ μὲν γὰρ οὐκ ὀφείλει κατακαλύπτεσθαι τὴν κεφαλήν, εἰκὼν καὶ δόξα θεοῦ ὑπάρχων· ἡ γυνὴ δὲ δόξα ἀνδρός ἐστιν, **we learn that to the direct subjection of the man to Christ corresponds the fact that the man is** εἰκὼν καὶ δόξα θεοῦ**, and to the position of man as** κεφαλή **of the** γυνή **corresponds the fact that she is the** δόξα ἀνδρός. (bold emphasis mine)

Kittel, Gerhard, Geoffrey William. Bromiley, and Gerhard Friedrich. Theological Dictionary of the New Testament. Vol. 3. Grand Rapids, MI: Eerdmans, 1964. 679. Print.

Zodhiates

In *The Complete Word Study Dictionary: New Testament*, Zodhiates writes that *kephale* is applied:

> (II) **Metaphorically of persons, i.e., the head, chief, one to whom others are subordinate, e.g., the husband in relation to his wife (1 Cor. 11:3**; Eph. 5:23) insofar as they are one body (Matt. 19:6; Mark 10:8), **and one body can have only one head to direct it** (bold emphasis mine).

Zodhiates, Spiros. The Complete Word Study Dictionary: New Testament. Chattanooga, TN, U.S.A.: AMG, 2000. Electronic edition.

Burke further mentions that the Lidell-Scott lexicon was the only lexicon that possibly suggested the meaning of "source" for *kephale*. He points to the following lexicons.

88. See BAGD 430; Louw-Nida, 1:739 ; also the older lexicons by Thayer, 345, and Craemer, 354; also TDNT 3:363–372; as well as **the sixth German edition of Walter Bauer**, Griechisch-deutsches Wšrterbuch (Berlin and New York: de Gruyter, 1988) 874-875; and most recently **A Greek-English Lexicon of the Septuagint (ed. J. Lust, E. Eynikel, and K. Hauspie**; Stuttgart: Deutsche Bibelgesellschaft, 1996) 254; similarly, for the patristic period **see Lampe, Patristic Greek Lexicon 749, as cited above**, ibid., p. 61. (bold emphasis mine)

xxiii Psalms 119:67

xxiv Psalms 119:71.

xxv Deuteronomy 8:2, 16; Job 1:1-12

xxvi *Blasphemeo* βλασφημέω **Strong's Number**: 987; Spoken of as evil, blaspheme, honored, hurling abuse, malign, revile, slander.

xxvii Don't confuse the newer tradition of mutual submission which is based upon the "precepts of men" with *hupotasso* (a woman's voluntary submission) which is based upon the commandments of God.

xxviii In the first century actors were called hupokrites (ὑποκριτής), from which we get the English word hypocrite. These actors often wore masks to help them pretend to be someone else. In this passage the hypocrites were acting, pretending to obey God's Word when, in fact, they were writing their own rules and doing and saying whatever they wanted.

xxix `*Etsem*, עֶצֶם **Strong's Number:** 6106; bone, essence, substance

xxx "You husbands in the same way, live with your wives in an understanding way [*gnosis*], as with someone weaker [*poieo*], since she is a woman; and show her honor as a fellow heir of the grace of life, so that your prayers will *not* be hindered."

xxxi Literally, as with a "weaker vessel."

xxxii Even in the English language, "husband," akin to "husbandry" and "groom," or "grooming" share the idea of nurturing the wife.

CHAPTER 2—The Business of Heaven

xxxiii Just what is the public square? In a phrase, it's the marketplace of "goods" and "ideas." In the last chapter, we learned how God's wisdom is expressed in the "marketplace of ideas." This chapter will concentrate on how God's wisdom is expressed in the "marketplace of goods."

xxxiv Or using 10 1/3 ounces/pound as they did in Jesus' time it would be roughly $15 million, $6 million, and $3 million.

xxxv *Oikodespotes*, οἰκοδεσπότης, Strong's Number: 3617; master of the house, householder.

xxxvi Genesis 31:7, Exodus 1:14, Leviticus 19:13, Deuteronomy 25:13-16,

2 Chronicles 10:4. Job 31:13,14, Proverbs 3:27, 11:1, 16:8, Jeremiah 22:13 Malachi 3:5, Ephesians 6:9, Colossians 4:1, 1 Timothy 5:18

xxxvii Luke 14:28-30

xxxviii Proverbs 27:23

xxxix Genesis 2:15, Proverbs 10:4-5; 12:14, 24; 13:4; 14:23; 18:9; 21:5; 28:19; Nehemiah 4:6, Ecclesiastes 9:10, Colossians 3:23; Romans 12:8

xl Proverbs 13:11, Ecclesiastes 11:1-2

xli Proverbs 15:22, 20:18, Proverbs 19:2 Proverbs 22:26-27 Ephesians 6:5-8.

xlii Matthew 15:15, 19, Proverbs 22:29

xliii Proverbs 27:23, Proverbs 27:26

xliv Proverbs 15:22, 20:18

xlv Genesis 2:15; Proverbs 12:14; Ecclesiastes 9:10; Nehemiah 4:6

xlvi Proverbs 19:2; 22:26-27; Ephesians 6:5-8

xlvii Proverbs 24:27; Ecclesiastes 11:2. I'm not sure if the third investor was choosing leisure once he abdicated his responsibility, but he certainly would have had the opportunity too. He was, at the very least, investing in idleness over the engine of production.

xlviii Proverbs 28:20. The third investor's decision was certainly hasty. Even if he had deliberated about it for a long time, he did so in a superficial way. It certainly shows a lack of truly considering other options.

xlix John 6:12. This can be applied to our third guy. He wastes his business manager's $4.6 million (not earning interest, thus losing potential earnings), his business manager's time (not only does his boss spend time entrusting him with the 1 talent, he also has to spend time admonishing him), and his own time as well.

l Deut. 8:18, 11:13—15; Eccl. 5:19; Neh. 6:9. How apt this advice is. If he was indeed evil, then prayer would be the exact antidote for it. In fact, the Lord's Prayer, specifically mentions this act—praying to be delivered from the evil that characterizes the 3rd investor. Also James 4:13-14.

li Deut. 24:19; 30:8-10; Joshua 1:8; Prov. 11:24-25; Psalms 1:1-3; 37:4; Nehemiah 2:20. This would include observing God's commandments, giving what is justly due, and being generous and compassionate.

lii Deuteronomy 25:13-15, Job 31:13-14, Proverbs 3:27, 11:1, Ephesians 6:9, Colossians 4:1

liii Leviticus 19:13, Job 31:13-14, Proverbs 3:27, Jeremiah 22:13, Malachi 3:5, James 5:4 1 Timothy 5:18

liv Proverbs 13:11, 16:8, 22:26, 1 Thessalonians 4:11

lv Exodus 22:14, Psalm 37:21, Proverbs 12:11

lvi Romans 13:7

lvii James 4:13,14

lviii Psalm 127:2, Ecclesiastes 5:12

lix This relationship is not necessarily symmetrical since never do we see the "kingdom of heaven" being used to describe business.

CHAPTER 3—In the Beginning (Part One)

lx http://www.gotquestions.org/falling-away.html

lxi Dr. Van Til focuses on this problem in his book *The Fourth Day*.

lxii So when does the Bible say that evening and morning begin?

> Evening: Mark 1:32 When evening came, after the <u>sun</u> had set…

> Morning: 2 Samuel 23:4 Is as the light of the morning when the <u>sun</u> rises…

Funny thing! When the Bible talks about evening and morning, there's going to be a sun in there some place.

lxiii "Face (surface) of the deep" in Proverbs 8:27 echoes Genesis 1:2. From the Proverbs passage we learn that "the surface of the deep" had to be already present for God to inscribe a circle on it (compare Isaiah 40:22). This absolutely refutes the SDC contention that the earth was present on the first day prior to the "surface of the deep."

lxiv Laird Harris, Gleason Archer, & Bruce Waltke, *Theological Wordbook of the Old Testament*, 1980
W.E. Vine, Merrill F. Unger, William White, *Vine's Complete Expository Dictionary* (Nashville, TN: Thomas Nelson Publishers, 1996), 54-55. Wayne Grudem, *Systematic Theology: An Introduction to Biblical Doctrine* (Grand Rapids, MI: Zondervan Publishing, 1994), 273, 290-291.9999

lxv See Appendix A.

lxvi While Dr. Sailhamer's work kindled my curiosity, my study reached very different conclusions.

lxvii This is found in footnote vii. Okay, for some of you this is a deal breaker. But before you close the book, go to Proverbs 1:22b.

"And scoffers delight themselves in scoffing..."

Now get a Strong's concordance and look at the Hebrew word translated "scoffers." It comes from the Hebrew word, *liyliyth*, referring to "Lilith," the name of a female goddess known as a night demon.

Why would translators translate *liyliyth* as "scoffers" when it clearly means something entirely different? The most likely reason is that they're trying to protect us from translations that may disturb us. Really...from whom? God? Sadly, I've found a number of these. The changes aren't so drastic as to affect our theology, but they are enough to reduce our access to God's truth. I'll get back to the *liyliyth* problem discussed here in a later chapter.

lxviii Even as school children we learn that time slows down as one approaches the speed of light.

lxix God's Clock is found in Isaiah, Lamentations, Ezekiel, Joel, Amos, Obadiah, Zephaniah, Malachi, Luke, Acts, 1 Corinthians, Philippians, Colossians, 1st and 2nd Thessalonians, 1st and 2nd Timothy, Titus, Hebrews, James, 1st and 2nd Peter, 1st John, Jude and Revelation.

lxx Many fairly ingenious attempts to resolve the text into Old Earth Creationism have included deconstructing the early church leaders, poetic or symbolic attributions, the infamous gap theory, Sailhamer's revisionist Genesis/promised land proposal, tranquil flood, local flood, Genesis as myth borrowing from ANE texts, noetic environment with *chronos* and *chairos* time, special hermeneutics for Genesis 1, God "lisping", framework theology, fog canopy (how could a fog obscure the sun from the earth when the earth wasn't even created until the third day?) and more recently "concordism," replacing the material description with a functional one.

Critics have examined all these proposals and found them wanting. They claim that each, in turn, has done damage to the clear teaching of the text.

^{lxxi} Yesterday in Man's Clock would be 24 hours while a "watch in the night" might vary between four and six hours. http://www.torahcalendar.com/HOUR.asp

^{lxxii} *Yom* יוֹם **Strong's Number:** 3117; day, time, year, day (as opposed to night), day (24 hour period), as defined by evening and morning in Genesis 1, as a division of time, a working day, a day's journey, days, lifetime (pl.), time, <u>period (general)</u>, year, temporal references, today, yesterday, tomorrow.

^{lxxiii} God's word teaches us that His power is often hidden in natural events as illustrated in James 1:16-17.

> "Do not be deceived, my beloved brethren. Every good thing given and every perfect gift is from above, coming down from the Father of lights, with whom there is no variation or shifting shadow."

^{lxxiv} Some Seven Day Creationists insist there was no rain before the flood. We know that that's not true since plants of the field are specifically mentioned after the curse almost 1500 years before the flood (Genesis 3:18).

^{lxxv} Hebrews 11:3 ... BY THE WORD OF GOD so that what is seen was not made out of things which are visible, 2 Peter 3:5 ... BY THE WORD OF GOD the heavens existed long ago and the earth was formed out of "water" and by "water", N.B. the Bible twice uses "water" elsewhere to describe gaseous particles

^{lxxvi} Isaiah 42:5, 51:13, Jeremiah 10:12.

^{lxxvii} Isaiah 42:5, 51:13, Jeremiah 10:12

CHAPTER 4—In the Beginning (Part Two)

^{lxxviii} Mathematically: cp Daniel 12:1-7 with vv 11,12, also 8:14, Revelation 11:3, 13:5 cp Revelation 12:6 and 12:14

^{lxxix} David Hume believes this argument fails because it is "a priori," a fancy way of saying that it is "outside of anyone's experience." Maybe it's outside of Hume's experience, but not God's. With Gottfried Leibniz, I'd ask Hume: "Why is there something rather than nothing?" Paraphrasing Hume's dilemma: In the beginning, there was nothing. Then nothing exploded…and there was everything.

We may also ask why we should listen to Hume, who was so

indoctrinated with the propaganda of empiricism that he denied that there was such a thing as cause-and-effect. Later Immanuel Kant showed that Hume's argument against causation (with his famous argument that there was no causal relationship between one billiard ball knocking another into a pocket) actually depended upon causes and effects being legitimate. Kant claimed that Hume needed to accept causality because Hume distinguished between event A (billiard ball 1 hitting ball 2) and event B (billiard ball 2 rocketing toward the pocket). Without causality, however, there would be no way to think of event A as separate from event B. Kant also argues that since the events are non-reversible (billiard ball 2 doesn't leap out of the pocket backwards towards the cue ball), event A must be the cause of event B.

For a more philosophical apologetic, read William Lane Craig's book *Come Let Us Reason.*

[lxxx] My personal interest was inflamed when the former Dean of Biological Sciences at the University of Minnesota told me not to apply to grad school because I was a Christian. The attitude of science toward people of faith is perverse. It is summarized in a statement from Richard Dawkins.

> "It is absolutely safe to say that if you meet somebody who claims not to believe in evolution, that person is ignorant, stupid or insane (or wicked, but I'd rather not consider that)."

My interest continued after I got into medical school. Though I'd doubt he'd remember, I had breakfast in California with one-time atheist, possible deist Michael Denton, who ironically started the intelligent design movement. I've dined with the Berkeley law professor emeritus Phillip Johnson and his wife, video-televised Michael Behe twice, made introductions with the astronomer Hugh Ross, visited polymer and design scientist Walter Bradley in his home, spoken at least twice by telephone to Jonathan Wells, put both Nancy Pearcey and Phillip Johnson on television, and am friends with author Walter Remine. I was invited to the International Mere Creation Conference in California. I even had a rare debate with an atheistic physics professor who was assisted by Bob Shadewald, former president of the National Center for

Science Education.

I know the meaning of big words like anthropic cosmological principle, noogenesis, ontogeny, speciation as well as little words like selfish gene and the red queen hypothesis. I've slept my way through various evolutionary advocates with their just-so story telling including Kevin Miller's argument from the human genome project using devolution to support evolution. Isn't it ironic when Miller and others observe evolution doing what it's not supposed to and conclude that this means evolution is true? Additionally, I've pondered my way through philosophical models using modus tollens and reverse falsifiability, negating the antecedent (theory of evolution) with falsified consequents (predictions). Even as a surgeon, I continue to read and have just under sixty academic books on the topic of evolution and of the origin of life.

Evolution has a long string of failed predictions including the zone of increasing complexity (fossils), failure of pre-biotic evolution, Provine's inept attempts to address Bradley's challenge to Gibb's energy equations, failed statistical models with pre/post-diction fallacies, collapse of Dawkin's blind watchmaker to the biotic message (simultaneously validating Paley's Watchmaker analysis), anti-intellectual challenges to Behe's irreducible complexity (amusingly distorting Behe which was then echoed by others, together with the spelling errors), and the ad baculum non-response to the Dembski Meyer filter.

lxxxi Taken from *Chance and Necessity: An Essay on the Natural Philosophy of Modern Biology* by Jacques Monod. I replaced "necessity" with "time" because in my mind it more accurately phrases the question.

lxxxii Proponents of evolution reject this. They claim that the expression "survival of the fittest" was unfortunate. They say it should be replaced by differential reproduction as a function of traits that have a genetic basis.

They argue that this updated formula creates the all-important independent criteria required to make it a scientific statement. They like to use words like improved design, heritable characters, fitness, and reproductive success to make their case. The text explains why this makes no difference.

lxxxiii This is of course reductive since evolutionists would first propose a prebiotic soup, producing protocells, prokaryotypes, eukaryotypes, multiple iterations of single cell organisms leading to multiple cell organisms, and multiple iterations later primitive body forms as found in the Burgess Shale.

lxxxiv Please note that my explanation is complicated by current methods of classification. Presently much of the Linnaean system is replaced by cladism, systematics, and phylogenetics. Moreover, in an effort to address bacteria in all their forms there are now three Domains and six Kingdoms. None-the-less the points remain valid.

lxxxv The average "young earth" Christian is understandably confused about their own argument since Strong's Concordance defines (*miyn*) as "sometimes a species" and "descendants of the same ancestral gene pool" after which Strong's launches into a strong argument against evolution.

But Strong's definition is ironic given that genes were not even described until the middle of the 19th Century (by Gregor Mendel thousands of years after Adam and Eve). And the modern notion of species was not even understood until the 20th Century. Recently, John Wilkins described no fewer than 26 different ideas of what the word "species" even means. Given all that, does it seem reasonable that Strong's definition is what Moses meant in Genesis?
Source: RNCSE Volume 26 (4), 2006, "Species, Kinds, and Evolution," Reports of the National Center for Science Education, John Wilkins, University of Queensland, Page(s): 36–45.
(http://ncse.com/rncse/26/4/species-kinds-evolution)

lxxxvi The 26 variances between Genesis and various geologic proposals noticed by Dr. Terry Mortenson or the 33 from Richard Niessen are resolved or of no significance with overlapping days.

lxxxvii Given Ecclesiastes 3:11, it is probably not even biblical to insist that one particular explanation has to be God's plan.

> "He has made everything appropriate in its time. He has also set eternity in their heart, yet so that man will not find out the work which God has done from the beginning even to the end" (Ecclesiastes 3:11).

Meanwhile, reservations from the Dr. Gunn, the scholar (an SDC) who reviewed my Hebrew and Greek, will be available online for interested parties.

CHAPTER 5—The Soul and Make Believe

[lxxxviii] Dr. Bouma-Prediger uses "dust" as a short-hand for body ("formed dust").

[lxxxix] Bouma-Predinger, 2nd edition *For the Beauty of the Earth*, p. 66.

[xc] Bouma-Prediger believes the connections between *'Adam* and *'Adamah* confirm that the dirt is what makes us human (64). But similar sounding words don't necessarily imply anything special (parallel word construction fallacy). None-the-less this is exactly what Bouma-Prediger says: "We are humans because we are humus (dirt)..." (64).

[xci] 2nd Edition, p. 64, 88, 92 *For the Beauty of the Earth*.

[xcii] Bouma-Prediger emphasizes that the Covenant of Noah did not renew the authority given to man in Genesis 1:28 to "subdue and have dominion" over the earth. From this he claims that mankind no longer has stewardship over the animals. But Genesis 2:15 and 9:2 appear to contradict these claims.

Then the LORD God took the man and put him into the garden of Eden to cultivate it and keep it (Genesis 2:15).

That stewardship is continued in Genesis 9:2.

> "The fear of you and the terror of you will be on every beast of the earth and on every bird of the sky; with everything that creeps on the ground, and all the fish of the sea, into your hand they are given."

Dr. Bouma-Prediger dismissed Genesis 9:2 at the MacLaurin conference, saying that the "fear...and...terror" that animals feel is because humans have become meat eaters (Genesis 9:2-3).

[xciii] Bouma-Prediger claims that this new Noahic covenant is a kind of ecological manifesto between God and all the animals, including man. Quoting Bernhard Anderson, Bouma-Prediger says:

> "The Covenant of Noah, then, is universal in the widest

sense imaginable. It is fundamentally an ecological
covenant that includes not only human beings
everywhere but all animals..." (93).

Bouma-Prediger's contention is partly correct, the part of the covenant
where God says He won't again destroy the earth with water is between
God and <u>all</u> the animals. The rest of his contentions are based
upon...well, nothing. It calls on humans to repopulate the earth. It gives
authority of the animals to mankind, allowing humans conditionally to
eat meat. It documents the animals' fear of men and it demands capital
punishment for murder...nothing more, nothing less (Gen. 9).
[xciv] We're advised that "all the createds (sic) are related" (89) simply
because all are created on the same day. This, of course, is both logically
and factually wrong.

- Not all animals were created on the same day as humans.
- Even if you and a Pop-Tart were created on the same day it
  doesn't make you brother and sister.

Bouma-Prediger suggested (at a MacLaurin Ecology Conference at
which this book was promoted) that animals and humans are alike
because they both have *nephesh* (Hebrew for souls)...compare Gen. 2:7-
9, 9:12, compare Gen 1:26, 9:6, and 1 Cor. 15:39). The first part of
Bouma-Prediger's claim, i.e. that animals have *nephesh* is correct. But
whether animals have souls is uncertain since this word can also be
translated as living creatures. Regardless, his conclusion that man and
animals are alike doesn't necessarily follow. In this regard, 1 Cor. 15:39
says:

> "All flesh is not the same flesh, but there is one flesh of
> men, and another flesh of beasts, and another flesh of
> birds, and another of fish."

This becomes convoluted because in Bouma-Prediger's faulty non-
dualistic worldview, "flesh" <u>is</u> the soul. In fact, at the MacLaurin
seminar he consistently replaced "soul" with "flesh". Thus, by the law of
substitution this passage would read: "all "soul" is not the same

"soul"…thereby negating his claim.

^{xcv} Man is no longer preeminent as steward and is replaced by God at the center of creation (93-103).

^{xcvi} Dr. Bouma-Prediger's non-dualistic view of man seems designed to knock man off his pedestal. But could it be that it was God who placed humanity on this "pedestal"; the pedestal representing God's charge of stewardship (Genesis 2:5, 9:2b) "entrust[ing]" man from the very beginning to honor and protect His creation?

^{xcvii} The earth will never be destroyed; instead it will be renewed (68-71).

^{xcviii} We are asked to believe that 2 Pet 3:10 (NAS) was mistranslated. Rather than the earth being burned up, Bouma-Prediger thinks that the passage should read: "that the earth would be healed" (68-71, 107, 118).

> "But the day of the Lord will come like a thief, in which the heavens will pass away with a roar and the elements will be destroyed with intense heat, and the earth and its works will be burned up."

To his credit, Bouma-Prediger opines that even if it were to be burned up, that would still be no excuse for man to abuse the earth. Nonetheless, Bouma-Prediger still asks us to accept that this passage should have been translated to mean that the earth would undergo a kind of renewal.

Indeed, that reading would suit Bouma-Prediger's view of non-dualistic man and by extension man's non-dualistic relationship with nature. But Second Peter is not the only passage with something to say. In Matthew 24:5 we read that the entire universe will pass away. Again in Revelation 21:1 we find that the earth will exist no longer. And finally in 2 Peter 3:12 "the heavens will be destroyed by burning, and the elements will melt with intense heat." "Destroyed" comes from the Greek *luo* and means that "parts of the universe will be broken up and destroyed"; "burning" comes from "*puroo*" meaning "to burn with fire," "heat" from "*kausoo*" meaning "to burn up."

> "Looking for and hastening the coming of the day of God, because of which the heavens will be destroyed by burning, and the elements will melt with intense heat." (2nd Peter

3:12)

Regardless of how this passage is translated, I agree with Dr. Bouma-Prediger's default position that it does not excuse abuse of God's creation. At the same time, it would be difficult to see how dualism would be invalidated by either translation.

[xcix] (Chapter 5, 2nd ed).

[c] Dr. Richard J. Mouw, Ph.D., former president of Fuller Theological Seminary (1993–2013), presently Distinguished Professor of Faith and Public Life. Question: How is it that this PhD trained philosopher did not recognize and address these issues with Dr. Bouma-Prediger prior to the book's publication? Bouma-Prediger's theme of man as steward of God's creation would have found fertile soil in the Bible without invoking non-biblical teachings of non-dualism.

[ci] The trinity of spirit and soul and body is a far deeper discussion beyond the scope of this chapter. If the reader wants to pursue that he might begin with 1 Thessalonians 5:23

[cii] Bouma-Prediger might argue that he was misunderstood. If so, why does Dr. Bouma-Prediger repeat this over and over in his book? Read in context I believe they reinforce Bouma-Prediger's contempt for "Creation denying dualisms dividing man and earth" (p. 66, 2nd ed.).

1. "The emphasis within the Christian tradition on dualisms of soul and body, spirit and matter, denigrate the earth and sanctions its misuse and exploitation." (p. 60-61, 2nd ed.)
2. Bouma-Prediger uses the quote above to introduce five authors, all of whom claim that Christian dualism rapes the earth.
3. Bouma-Prediger then argues that these five authors are wrong about Christianity because it is not dualistic as they assume. He claims that the Bible never teaches that there is a spirit separate from the body (66).
4. Bouma-Prediger's earth friendly "ecological motif" also rejects the idea of a separate "spirit and matter (body/dust)" (66).
5. "The initial premise is unacceptable— the claim that the Bible promotes a dualism between soul and body, spirit and

matter…" (p. 66, 2nd ed.).

[ciii] Dr. Bouma-Prediger used quotes/shadow quotes to make his points. This allows him to use others to say things for him. Meticulous re-reads of his book confirms these are his thoughts.

[civ] *Ruwach* חוּר **Strong's Number:** 7307; wind, breath, mind, spirit, breath, spirit (as that which breathes quickly in animation or agitation); spirit (of the living, breathing being in man and animals); never referred to as a de-personalized force.

[cv] The question of death gives Dr. Bouma-Prediger a second, potentially more embarrassing problem. When we die the dust is no longer animated. But remember, in Dr. Bouma-Prediger's world the soul is really just "living dust." There is no soul or spirit which could then "return to God." Consequently, the only people with "souls" who could go to heaven would be those still alive when Jesus returns. Everybody else would just be lumps of dirt left to be reabsorbed into the earth.

[cvi] *`Aphar* רָפָע **Strong's Number:** 6083; dry earth, dust, powder, ashes, earth, ground, mortar, rubbish.

[cvii] Their contention has a striking parallel to the French philosopher Derrida's claim that binary oppositions (i.e. dualisms) create a violent hierarchy as one exploits the other. But the dogma that dualisms are inherently evil is unsupported. For this proof recall that God is spirit.

> "God is spirit, and those who worship Him must worship in spirit and truth" (John 4:24).

God, who is spirit, created the physical world. But God who is spirit does not denigrate the world. He doesn't misuse it. And He doesn't exploit it. He calls it good.

[cviii] The first monarch of Israel learned this when he was removed as king because of his disobedience (1 Samuel 13:13-14).

[cix] The scholar reviewing my Hebrew, Dr. Gunn, says about Genesis 9:2 "into your hand they are given *(nathan)*. Context is the key here. The verb *nathan* in the *Niph'al* stem: the idea is probably "given under one's authority," which comes close to "entrusted" but has a slightly different connotation.

CHAPTER 6—Minding the Brain

[cx] Swahili for motorcycle.

[cxi] The neurologist confirmed that there never was a fracture. Instead the young boy's paralysis was caused by a bruise on his brain stem. The boy recovered completely.

[cxii] *Nephesh* **Strong's Number:** 5315; נֶפֶשׁ soul, self, life, creature, person, appetite, <u>mind,</u> living being, desire, emotion, passion, that which breathes, the breathing substance or being, soul, the inner being of man, the man himself, self, person or individual, seat of the appetites, seat of emotions and passions, <u>activity of the mind,</u> activity of the will, activity of the character. (bold emphasis mine)

[cxiii] Descartes believed that the mind controlled the brain, much like a ghost operating a machine. He was sure the command center was in the pineal gland. He said the soul was a ghost in a machine. So how could something non-physical, i.e. a soul, pull its levers or push buttons? How could it make the brain tell the body to go?

Knowing how we know has always intrigued scientists. Philosophers generally answer this question in one of two ways. Some believe only that the mind is real. They are called idealists. They only believe ideas, that is, products of the mind, are real. The other philosophers are the ones we are dealing with in this chapter: the materialists. They reject the idea of the mind entirely. You don't need a ghost/mind to run the machine/brain. The machine/brain can run itself. For them, talking about the mind, or soul or inner mental states, is unscientific.

Rejecting the idea that we even need a ghost in the machine is a very natural next step for scientists and philosophers. That's because they believe that the machine/brain explains all of our thoughts and actions without ever having to invoke a ghost/soul.

[cxiv] Wittgenstein used this example to say that our subjective sensations aren't meaningful unless those subjection sensations can be learned through public experience and discussed via a publicly-known language (i.e. looking inside our own private boxes couldn't be the criteria we used to find out what a beetle was. That's because each person could have something entirely different in their box, or the content of the box could constantly change, or the box could be empty). Wittgenstein's argument can be used to deny that we have private mental states. This is

very similar to our mind/brain debate, and private mental states can be thought of as another term for the mind. I find the beetle a helpful image for our mind/brain issue.

cxv Even though Chalmers rejected all nine versions of materialism, he still remained convinced that materialism was correct (although he doesn't provide a good reason for this). Jeff Schwartz wryly dubbed Chalmer's view "don't have a clue" materialism.

cxvi Former editor in chief of the magazine *Science*.

cxvii I applaud Dr. Schwartz who challenged the robot iconography because his Buddhist beliefs embrace "free will" as a cause of action producing Karma. This is a reprimand to Christians who adjust their beliefs to the current fashion of materialism.

> "I say this to your shame. Is it so, that there is not among you one wise man who will be able to decide between his brethren" (1 Corinthians 6:5).

cxviii *Didaskalia* (διδασκαλία) **Strong's Number:** 1319; teaching, instruction, doctrine.

cxix The Greek word *elegxis*, translated "reproof," is seen over and over in the arguments recorded in the early Greek judicial system.

It seems that Athenians would regularly take their neighbors to court. But before they went they would hire a "rhetorician" who would argue their case. Today, Greek profs condemn their poor students to study those cases where they routinely find the word *elegxis*. It was used to say that the evidence absolutely proves the other party wrong, without exception.

Elegsis ἔλεγξις **Strong's Number:** 1649; refutation, rebuke.

cxx *Epanothosis* ἐπανόρθωσις **Strong's Number:** 1882; restoration to an upright or right state, correction, improvement of life or character.

cxxi This doesn't minimize the importance of the Holy Spirit in this activity. That is just a different conversation.

cxxii *Paideia* παιδεία: **Strong's Number:** 3809; "training," whatever cultivates the soul, especially by correcting mistakes and curbing passions; instruction which aims at increasing virtue.

CHAPTER 7—Hope and Change

cxxiii "Biblical hope" is very different from the "hope-so hope" we use in day-to-day conversations. Biblical hope, used by God to describe Himself (Romans 15:13) is that of "confident expectation."

cxxiv "The word "righteous", a neologism created by Tyndale, comes from the Old English: *rihtwīs (right + wise)*. MSWorks dictionary. But I wonder: what is right and who is wise?

Beyt Shimon suggests that abstract words are best understood through their original concrete root. To understand *tsadaq* translated righteousness, we should look at the noun *tsadiyq* which means "a straight line." *Tsadaq*, then, would be "walking a straight line") or figuratively "what is right" which is where we get the words "right" and "righteous." Shimon, Beyt HaKakosh http://www.therefinersfire.org/torah_and_righteousness.htm

cxxv *Tsadaq* צָדַק **Strong's Number:** 6663; to be just, be righteous; to have a just cause, be in the right; to be justified.

cxxvi Also 48:22; 57:2; and Psalms 34:14.

cxxvii *Rules for Radicals* is a book by Saul Alinsky: "Lest we forget at least an over-the-shoulder acknowledgment to the very first radical: from all our legends, mythology, and history (and who is to know where mythology leaves off and history begins — or which is which), the first radical known to man who rebelled against the establishment and did it so effectively that he at least won his own kingdom — Lucifer."

cxxviii Lest you think envy is benign, consider that scripture says they delivered Jesus up because of envy (Matthew 27:18).

cxxix As an exercise, compare the Exodus 18:21 man of truth in government with Alinsky's expedient morality.

cxxx *Meyshar* מֵישָׁרִים **Strong's Number:** 4339; evenness, uprightness, straightness, equity, evenness, level, smoothness, uprightness, equity.

cxxxi *Chokmah* הָמְכָה **Strong's Number:** 2451; wisdom, skill (in war), wisdom (in administration), shrewdness, wisdom, wisdom, prudence (in religious affairs), wisdom (ethical and religious).

cxxxii *Encarta ® World English Dictionary* © & (P) 1998-2005 Microsoft Corporation. All rights reserved.

cxxxiii Interesting Christian discussion of vocation at: http://www.princeton.edu/~aia/files/vbc/Vocations_and_Calling.pdf

CHAPTER 8—Fools and their Folly

cxxxiv Proverbs 12:23, 13:16, 14:24, 15:2, 15:14, 15:21, 16:22, 17:12, 24:9, 26:4, 26:5, 26:11, also 1 Samuel 25:25, Ps 53:1, Eccl 10:12,13.

cxxxv Other nuances include "young, inexperienced, easily seduced."

cxxxvi *Pethiy* יְתֹם **Strong's Number:** 6612; simplicity, naivete, simple, foolish, open-minded.

cxxxvii *'Eviyl* לִיְוֶא **Strong's Number:** 191; be foolish, foolish, (subst), of one who despises wisdom, of one who mocks when guilty, of one who is quarrelsome, of one who is licentious.

cxxxviii *Latsown* וְצָל **Strong's Number:** 3944; scorning, bragging.

cxxxix *Liyliyth* תיִלְיִל **Strong's Number:** 3917; "Lilith", name of a female goddess known as a night demon who haunts the desolate places of Edom.

cxl *Keciyl* לִיסַכ **Strong's Number:** 3684; fool, stupid fellow, dullard, simpleton, arrogant one.

cxli Proverbs 1:22 (hate knowledge), 32 (live in ease and prosperity), 3:35 (dishonorable), 8:5 (need wisdom), 10:1 (grieves mother), 10:18 (spread slander), 12:23 (proclaim folly), 13:16 (display folly), 13:19-20 (abomination to turn from evil, companions suffer harm), 14:7-8 (will deceitfully lead you away from knowledge), 14:16 (arrogant, careless), 14:24 (demonically influenced: *'ivveleth*), 15:2 (speech demonically influenced: *'ivveleth*), 15:14 (demonically feeds on folly: *'ivveleth*), 15:20 (despises mother), 17:10 (refuse correction), 17:12 (demonically dangerous), 17:16 (have money, but no sense), 17:24-25 (eyes are on the ends of the earth, possibly his interests are aligned with the world), 18:2 (not interested in understanding, only in his own heart, mind, thinking, view of the world), 18:6-7 (speech leads to quarrels), 19:1 (have no integrity, twisted, perverse), 21:20 (swallow up the treasure of the wise), 23:9 (despises wisdom), 26:6,10 (unreliable, treacherous to employers), 28:26 (trusts their own heart), 29:11 (cannot control temper), Eccl 2:14 (walk in darkness), 4:5 (lazy), 5:3,4 (spiritually empty, prayer without action), 7:4-6 (addicted to pleasure), 7:9 (angry), 10:12 (own speech swallows him up), 10:15 (worn out by his own folly).

cxlii *Eklektos* ἐκλεκτός **Strong's Number:** 1588; picked out, chosen, the Messiah, as appointed by God to the most exalted office conceivable.

cxliii From Proverbs 1:32, "…And the complacency of [*keciyl*] will destroy them. "Complacency" is translated from the Hebrew *shalvah* meaning complacency, ease, prosperity, quietness, and time of tranquility.

^{cxliv} *Naval* לְבָנ **Strong's Number:** 5036; foolish, senseless, fool.

CHAPTER 9—Mirror, Mirror, On the Wall

^{cxlv} The rest of the bald area grew back with normal thickness. Only "where the thing was" (like my prayer) grew in twice as thick. Sometimes God "helps" our weak faith by showing us His power even when our prayers are frivolous.

^{cxlvi} A misreading of Matthew 7 which is really about judgment correctly exercised.

^{cxlvii} Of course, that's the figure of speech fallacy. Unless they literally meant that your head had to be physically thin to squeeze into a narrow pathway, and then it would just be weird. More likely, they meant the former (figure of speech fallacy) in which case they're not going to understand logical argument anyway.

^{cxlviii} "Tu Quogue" is French for "you say." It is used to represent an error in thinking. For example, you tell me I am ugly and I say, "You mean you are."

^{cxlix} *`Ormah* הַמְרָע, **Strong's Number:** 6195; shrewdness, craftiness, prudence.

^{cl} There are actually two different kinds of "shrewdness" found in Proverbs. `*Ormah*, the one I just mentioned, is simply given to the naïve: "The proverbs of Solomon the son of David, king of Israel: To know wisdom and instruction, To discern the sayings of understanding, To receive instruction in wise behavior, Righteousness, justice and equity; <u>to give (*Nathan*) prudence (`*ormah*) to the naïve</u>" (Proverbs 1:1-3a; bold emphasis mine).

The second type of prudence is *sakal*. Strong's defines *sakal* (#7919) as the following: to be prudent, be circumspect, wisely understand, prosper.

Sakal includes shrewdness, but also encompasses circumspection and insight. Moreover, it is something we get as we <u>ponder and practice</u> shrewd behavior: "The proverbs of Solomon the son of David, king of Israel: To know wisdom and instruction, To discern the sayings of understanding, <u>to receive instruction in wise (*sakal*) behavior</u>…" (Proverbs 1:1-3a, compare Hebrews 5:14).

"Instruction" comes from the Hebrew (*musar*) and means a discipline, chastening, or correction. *Sakal* is giving attention to this discipline in wise behavior.

Or said another say, '*ormah* is simple understanding of shrewd behavior, whereas *sakal* is shrewdness, circumspection, and insight obtained from thoughtful practice.

[cli] *Phronimos* is the practically wise man, one who has *phronesis* (practical wisdom or shrewdness). Aristotle claims that both practical wisdom (*phronesis*) and theoretical wisdom (*sophia*) are necessary to know the highest wisdom (which is knowledge of causes). This is because *phronesis* (practical wisdom) is required to make observations. *Sophia*, or theoretical wisdom, reasons from these observations to make a governing statement. For example, from *phronesis* we might observe the sun rising every day for a year. Then using *sophia* we can reason that the sun will <u>always</u> rise in the morning.

[clii] Remember that the Old Testament was written in Hebrew while the New Testament is written in Greek. So when we turn to the New Testament we find that "shrewdness" is translated from the Greek word, *phronimos*.

[cliii] 5th Edition.

[cliv] Koehler & Baumgartener suggest "cleverness."

[clv] These were non-statistical averaging of three separate studies reported by Brett Kunkle at Conversant Life. Obviously the question and the number and type of participants varied in each group.

[clvi] A fourth study of teens in 2003 by Barna was even more disturbing…only one teen in twenty believed the Bible (regarding accuracy; salvation by grace; Biblical view of God, Jesus, and Satan; and Jesus' command to evangelize).

[clvii] Psalms 107:17; Proverbs 1:7; 7:22; 10:8; 12:15-16; 14:9; 15:5; 20:3; 27:3; 29:9.

[clviii] "Therefore let him who thinks he stands take heed that he does not fall." (1 Corinthians 10:12).

[clix] Also in Proverbs 1:1, 2, 5, 6

[clx] *Mezimmah* מְזִמָּה **Strong's Number:** 4209; purpose, discretion, device, plot.

[clxi] This is reinforced in Galatians 5:14:

"For the whole Law is fulfilled in one word, in the statement,
"YOU SHALL LOVE YOUR NEIGHBOR AS YOURSELF.""

clxii Psalm 92:6, 94:8, Proverbs 1:22,32, 8:5, 10:18, 12:23, 13:20, 14:8, 16, 17:10, 24, 18:2,6,7, 19:1, 21:20, 23:9, 26:4,5, 29:11,20, Ecclesiastes 2: 14-16, 4:5,13, 5:1,3,4, 7:9, 10:2,12,15

clxiii Liberties taken since the original quote was from Sartre, and the actual words of Dostoevsky's character were different.

clxiv Time Magazine, October 31, 1994 "Infidelity – It May Be In Our Genes"

clxv Footnote:Alfred Rahlfs, ed., *Septuaginta*, 7th ed. (Stutgart: Wurtenbergische Bibelanstalt, 1962.

clxvi New World Dictionary: Eon: Period of immense duration; an age; endless; for eternity.

Webster's Collegiate Dictionary: *Eon* (n.): An immeasurable or indefinite period of time; incessantly; synonym of constantly, continuously, always, perpetually, unceasingly, everlastingly, endlessly.

Standard Unabridged Dictionary: *Eon*: An age of the universe; an incalculable period, constituting one of the longest conceivable divisions of time; a cosmic or geological cycle; an eternity, or eternity. The present age, or eon, is time; the future age, or eon, is eternity.

Shedd Theological Dictionary (vol. II, p. 683): *Eonian*: pertaining to, or lasting for eons; everlasting; eternal.

Liddell and Scott's Greek-English Lexicon: *Aion*: A period of existence; one's lifetime; life; an age; a generation; a long space of time; an age. A space of time clearly defined and marked out; an era, epoch, age, period or dispensation.

Thesaurus Dictionary of the English Language: *Eon*: An age of the universe.

Earnest Weekly's Etymological Dictionary of Modern English: *Aeon*: Age.

Universal Dictionary: *Aeon*: A period of immense duration; an age.

Thayer's Greek-English Lexicon: *Aionios*: (1) without beginning or end; that which has been and always will be. (2) without beginning. (3) without end, never to cease, everlasting.

Encyclopedic Dictionary of the Bible: In the N.T., *aion* is used as the equivalent of *olam*. The Hebrew word *olam*, which is used alone (Ps. 61:8) or with various prepositions (Ge. 3:22; 13:15, etc.) in contexts where it is traditionally translated "forever," means, in itself, no more than "for an indefinitely long period." Thus, *me-olam* does not mean "from eternity," but "of old" (Ge 6:4).

The New Testament in Modern Speech, by Dr. R. F. Weymouth: *aeonion*," i.e., "of the ages." Etymologically this adjective, like others similarly formed, does not signify "during," but "belonging to" the *aeons* or ages.

The Interpreter's Dictionary of the Bible (vol. IV, p. 643): The word *aion* originally meant "vital force," "life;" then "age," "lifetime." It is, however, also used generally of a (limited or unlimited) long space of time. The use of the word *aion* is determined very much by the O.T. and the LXX. *Aion* means "long distant uninterrupted time" in the past (Luke 1:10), as well as in the future (John 4:14).

Ellicott's Commentary on the Whole Bible (Matt. 25:46): *aionios*-it must be admitted (1) that the Greek word which is rendered "eternal" does not, in itself, involve endlessness, but rather, duration, whether through an age or succession of ages, and that it is therefore applied in the N.T. to periods of time that have had both a beginning and ending (Rom. 16:25), where the Greek is "from *aeonian* times;" our version giving "since the world began." (Comp. 2 Tim. 1:9; Tit. 1:3) -strictly speaking, therefore, the word, as such, apart from its association with any qualifying substantive, implies a vast undefined duration, rather than one in the full sense of the word "infinite."

Triglot Dictionary of Representative Words in Hebrew, Greek and English [this dictionary lists the words in this order: English, Greek, Hebrew] (p. 122): Eternal (see age-lasting). (p. 6): English: age-lasting; Greek, *aionios*; Hebrew, *le-olam*.

[203]

A Greek-English Lexicon, by Arndt and Gingrich: (1) *Aion*: time; age; very long time; eternity. (2) A segment of time; age. (3) The world. (4) The *aion* as a person: *aionios*, eternal. 1. Without beginning. 2. Without beginning or end. 3. Without end.

Manual Greek Lexicon of the New Testament, by Abbott-Smith: *Aion*: A space of time, as a lifetime, generation, period of history, an indefinitely long period-an age, eternity.